CULTIVATING GRATITUDE

....

THE KEY TO A LIFE OF PEACE AND PURPOSE

JESSE, A SERVANT OF CHRIST

I0560716

Covenant Ministries of Texas, Inc
Royse City, Texas

Publishing
Covenant Ministries of Texas, Inc
6376 State Hwy 276 W
Royse City, Texas 75189
https://covenantministiestx.org

Book Layout ©2017 BookDesignTemplates.com

Ordering Information:
Quantity sales. Special discounts are available on quantity purchases by corporations, associations, and others. For details, contact the "Special Sales Department" at the address above.

Book Title Cultivating Gratitude, The Key to a Life of Peace and Purpose. Author jesse, a servant of Christ. . -- 1st ed.
ISBN 979-8-89778-545-2

Contents

Dedication..ix

Preface..xiii

Introduction:..xvi

Chapter One:..1

The Quiet Heart..1

    A Heart Set on Gratitude....................................5

Chapter Two:..11

A Heart of Thanksgiving in the Word of God

....11

Chapter Three:..21

The Practice of Presence and Gratitude..........21

    Mindfulness as a Path to Gratitude.............23

    The Grateful Heart...25

    The Practice of Gratitude in Daily Life.......27

    Cultivating Gratitude..28

Chapter Four:..33

Expressing Gratitude to Others........................33

    Gratitude for Kingdom-Minded Givers......35

    Gratitude in the Workplace.............................37

    Gratitude as a Lifelong Practice....................44

Chapter Five: 47

The Transformative Power of a Grateful Heart
....47

Chapter Six: 55

The Practice of Mindful Reflection in
Gratitude..55

The Power of Guided Reflection and
Contemplation..58

Simple Daily Practices for Mindful
Gratitude 61

Gratitude as a Journey of Faith.................... 66

Chapter Seven: The Sacred Union of
Gratitude and Prayer................................... 69

Beginning Prayer with Thanksgiving......... 70

The Practice of Contemplative Prayer in
Gratitude 71

Intercessory Prayer Infused with Gratitude
....74

Scriptural Prayers of Thanksgiving..............77

Daily Acts of Thankful Prayer 79

Chapter Eight: 83

Removing Barriers to a Grateful Heart 83

Overcoming Guilt Through Grace................87

Letting Go of Shame and Embracing Self-Worth 88

Releasing Resentment Through Forgiveness 92

Chapter Nine: 93

Overcoming Depression with Gratitude 93

The Power of Affirmation in Cultivating Gratitude 96

The God of Promise, The God of Peace.... 99

A Powerful Resource 104

Chapter Ten: 107

Sustaining a Life of Gratitude 107

Making Gratitude a Daily Habit 109

Consistency: The Key to Lasting Practice.. 111

Surrounding Yourself with Gratitude Reminders.. 112

Chapter Eleven: 115

The Power of Gratitude in Action 115

The Heart Behind the Act................................ 116

Simple Acts, Lasting Impact........................... 117

Serving Without Expectation 118

Serving as an Expression of Faith 119

Acts of Service in Challenging Times 120

The Joy of Serving 121

Chapter Twelve: 123

The Reciprocal Nature of Gratitude 123

Gratitude Within Families: A Cycle of Love
.... 124

Gratitude in Friendships: Strengthening
Bonds 127

Gratitude in the Workplace: Fostering a
Culture of Appreciation 128

Gratitude and Our Relationship with God
.... 128

The Challenge of Accepting Gratitude 132

Receiving Help: A Strength, Not a
Weakness 133

Embracing the Full Circle of Gratitude 133

Chapter Thirteen: 135

The Bridge Between Gratitude and
Forgiveness 135

Acknowledging the Hurt: The First Step
Toward Healing 136

Shifting Perspective: Finding Gratitude in
the Midst of Pain 137

The Transformative Power of Empathy 138

Forgiveness Is a Gift We Give Ourselves. 139

Self-Forgiveness: Embracing Grace for Ourselves........................140

Walking in Freedom..........................141

Chapter Fourteen:..........................143

The Transformative Power of Gratitude in Relationships..........................143

Chapter Fifteen:..........................147

Building Resilience Through Gratitude.........147

Chapter Sixteen:..........................155

Living with Gratitude: A Life of Peace and Purpose..........................155

Chapter Seventeen:..........................161

A Life Marked by Gratitude..........................161

Acknowledgements:..........................167

ABOUT THE AUTHOR..........................171

Dedication

This book is dedicated to my dear baby sister, Diane—who, despite suffering many years with depression, remained faithful to Christ and never relinquished her hope in Him. Through faith, perseverance, and the grace of God, she eventually found healing. And with that healing came peace, purpose, and the rich blessings of a grateful heart. Today, Diane is a radiant beacon of gratitude and hope, unashamed to share her story in the prayerful hope that it might help someone else find the healing she now walks in.

Thank you, Di, for allowing me to share your struggle and your victory—the kind of victory only Christ can give.

When I sent Diane the excerpt from her chapter for review, she wanted to make a few things clear for the readers of this book. Rather than attempt to paraphrase her, I've included her full email below. (Forgive the reference to my writing—she is, after all, my baby sister.)

"Jesse, your writing is beautifully eloquent, & it seems that no matter the subject you write on, I am always happily surprised by your way with words. Having said that, for the sake of acknowledging mom & dad's deep love & care for us/me as their child(ren), I would preface this story with the fact that mother faithfully read the Bible to me when I was young, & patiently answered any questions that I had about God & the Bible. I remember feeling her love & affection towards me during these readings, & I credit her for the healing I received from God, because of her misguided discipline/punishment.

Also, as far as dad was concerned, the fact that he was such a loving & affectionate father to me helped in my receiving healing from God, in that, because I knew my earthly father was good & accepting of me, I knew that my heavenly Father was perfectly good & accepting of me.

Also, I think that it may be important to mention that Pa ████ was a step-grandfather. I have always been thankful that I didn't have to endure any of the violation from a biological grandfather. In my mind, it was one less injury to my soul & a mercy from God. Bottom line, I believe with all of my heart that mother & dad did the very best they could by me. Even in my very young years I knew that. It may have been the reason I never knew where to direct the burning anger in me. I hope this helps. Let me know if you have any questions."

Colossians 3:15-17:

"And let the peace of Christ rule in your hearts, to which indeed you were called in one body. And be thankful. Let the word of Christ dwell in you richly, teaching and admonishing one another in all wisdom, singing psalms and hymns and spiritual songs, with thankfulness in your hearts to God. And whatever you do, in word or deed, do everything in the name of the Lord Jesus, giving thanks to God the Father through him".

Preface

In the quiet hush of the heart—amidst the clamor of a world relentlessly chasing shadows—a simple truth whispers: *gratitude*.

This book was not born from a passing thought, but from a deep conviction. A conviction shaped by watching the sun rise over countless fields, by witnessing the patient unfolding of a single wildflower, and by finding solace in the stillness of a starlit night. It speaks to the transformative power of a grateful heart—not a power that merely feels good for a moment, but one that heals from within, touching the very fabric of who we are: mind, body, and spirit.

These words come from the heart of a man who, in the eyes of many, once had it all. But through the sin of pride, he squandered everything, and found himself alone and broken, lying on a narrow bunk in a federal prison. That bunk—a thin, two-inch plastic-covered pad atop half an inch of cold steel—became the unlikely altar where God's relentless, reckless grace met him. It was there, stripped of everything he once held dear, that he was wooed by love, embraced by mercy, and called to repentance.

And it was there, in that most humbling of places, that restoration began.

This book is an invitation to journey together—seeking a deeper understanding through the timeless wisdom of scripture and the shared stories of ordinary lives touched by grace. It is not merely an intellectual pursuit, but a pilgrimage of the soul. A practical guide for navigating life's winding paths with renewed wonder and heartfelt appreciation.

Together, we will listen for the ancient echoes of faith, and in scripture, we will find the heartbeat of gratitude—a heart open to divine love, a heart growing in grace, a heart learning to see God's hand in the details of daily life.

We will also face the shadows that try to dim the light: anxiety, depression, sorrow, and shame. But even there, we will discover how gratitude—like a persistent sunbeam—can pierce the darkness. We will uncover practical, faith-filled steps to cultivate peace, resilience, and joy.

This is a journey of self-discovery. A tender unfolding of the soul. A gradual awakening to the blessings that surround us—both grand and minuscule—like the morning dew on a summer field.

My deepest prayer is that these pages become a sanctuary for you. A place of refuge, inspiration, and gentle awakening. May they lead you toward a heart overflowing with gratitude—and toward a life richer, deeper, and more profoundly fulfilling than you ever imagined.

May this book be a gentle shepherd, guiding you to greener pastures... where peace and thanksgiving dwell.

Introduction:

GRATITUDE—WHERE DOES IT BEGIN?

Not long ago, I was on my way to the airport, driving a young lady who had been volunteering at the ministry here in Alaska. She was headed home to Germany, and during our two-hour journey, we talked about many things—including the differences between churches in Germany and those in the United States.

As she described the traditions and customs she was familiar with, I was taken aback. The church services she knew were formal and stoic. Women were not permitted to pray aloud in services, and there was an overwhelming lack of emotion in worship.

Having been raised in a Pentecostal or Charismatic tradition, where heartfelt praise and worship were deeply woven into every gathering, I struggled to understand such a setting. I shared that with her.

"I just don't understand how people can get emotional about church," Leah said gently.

Her words stopped me cold. I turned to her, stunned. "How can you not?" I asked. And then, without intending to, I found myself pouring out what had been buried in my heart all along.

I said, "Leah, consider this. If you truly believe that from the moment you were born—because you were born in sin, shaped in iniquity—your destiny was eternal damnation, an eternity separated from God... If you believe that God, in His unfathomable love, left the splendor of heaven—left the angels who bow before Him crying, 'Holy, Holy, Holy'— and came to earth to live a sinless life, the life you and I were incapable of living... If you believe He did this so that we might be reconciled to Him and join Him in glory...

"And while here, He was despised and rejected by His creation, the very people He came to save. He was beaten so that you could be healed, crucified so that His blood could purchase your salvation. He died one of the most horrific deaths imaginable— and then, He rose again so that you could have hope in life beyond death...

"If you really believe all of that—how can your heart not be overwhelmed with gratitude? How can that gratitude not grow into love, and that love not blossom into worship? Gratitude and love are not only choices—they're feelings, emotions, responses to a truth that cannot be ignored."

I glanced over and saw tears rolling down Leah's cheeks. She looked at me quietly and said, "I get it now."

That moment on the highway was sacred. Not because of the words I spoke, but because truth pierced through, touched her heart, and gratitude was born.

Pastor Tim Keller once said that Jesus left His glory—His treasure—to purchase us. We became His treasure. How much more, then, should He become the treasure of our hearts?

Jesus Himself said,

"Where your treasure is, there your heart will be also."

Gratitude begins the moment we recognize and acknowledge the great price that Jesus paid for our redemption. Even if He never provided another blessing—no healing, no breakthrough, no provision—what He did at Calvary would still be more than enough. His sacrifice alone warrants a lifetime of thankfulness.

Gratitude begins at the cross. And from there, it flows into every other part of our lives.

CHAPTER ONE:

THE QUIET HEART

A quiet heart overflowing with thankfulness holds a power that reaches far beyond mere appreciation. Gratitude is not just a pleasant sentiment; it is a deep, abiding wellspring, a gentle stream that nourishes both soul and body. The wise have always known this, and now even careful study confirms it, gratitude fosters a blossoming of well-being, bringing tangible renewal to how we think, feel, and live.

This is no fleeting notion, but a profound truth woven into the very fabric of our being. Consider the quiet messages that flow within us, shaping our moods and thoughts, influencing the rhythm of our days. A grateful heart gently nurtures these inner currents, fostering peace, contentment, and an enduring sense of calm. Imagine a stillness that settles within, a light that brightens even the darkest days, a strength that eases the burdens we carry. Gratitude is more than a mere reaction to blessings; it is a way of seeing, a posture of the heart that aligns our inner world with the goodness of God.

To cultivate gratitude is to cultivate resilience, to step into a life enriched with abiding peace. It is to recognize the beauty in simple things, to rejoice in small mercies, and to let joy sustain us in every season.

We've all heard the story of the eternal optimist, the young boy placed in a room full of manure by parents eager to temper his unrelenting hopefulness. When they checked on him, they found him digging eagerly, flinging manure aside with determination. "What on earth are you doing?" they asked. His response was simple and full of expectation: "With all this manure, there's got to be a pony in here somewhere!"

Such is the power of an unyielding attitude of gratitude. It shapes not just our outlook but our very experience of life. Even in hardship, gratitude shifts our perspective—from asking God why to asking what He is teaching us. It transforms trials into opportunities for growth, sorrow into a pathway for grace.

A grateful heart does not deny the presence of struggle, but it does declare that God's goodness is greater. In every circumstance, there is something to be learned, something to be cherished, and yes, even something to be thankful for.

The quiet hum of the earth, the gentle sway of meadow grasses—these are the whispers of creation that speak to me of gratitude's power. It's not just a passing thought or an occasional thankfulness; it is something far deeper, a way of seeing, a way of being. I have felt it in the warmth of the sun on my face, in the hush of the evening when the sky is painted in soft amber and gold. Gratitude is more than a response to good things—it is a posture of the heart, an openness to receive and recognize the blessings that surround us every day.

We all know what it's like to carry the weight of stress, that unseen burden pressing down, making each step feel heavier. It steals our peace, drains our joy, and leaves us weary. But gratitude is like a fresh wind stirring through the soul, loosening the grip of anxiety and lifting the weight from our shoulders. It is a quiet but powerful force, a counterbalance to the struggles we face. I have known moments when fear and uncertainty threatened to take root, yet when I turned my heart toward thanksgiving, even in the smallest ways, I found a refuge—a place of strength where peace could grow.

Gratitude does something remarkable; it settles the heart and quiets the mind. It turns our eyes from the worries of the day to the steady faithfulness of God. And when we rest in that, sleep comes more easily, our thoughts are less troubled, and our souls find stillness. It's no wonder that a heart steeped in gratitude rests more peacefully at night. When we make space for thanksgiving, our burdens feel lighter, and our hearts find rest.

But gratitude does not stop at bringing us peace, it changes the way we live. It shapes the way we see others, the way we respond to hardships, the way we press forward in faith. A thankful heart is a heart that sees beyond the immediate, that trusts in the goodness of God even when the road is difficult. And in that trust, there is joy. Not a fleeting happiness that comes and goes with circumstances, but a deep and abiding joy that holds us steady through every season.

Perhaps this is why gratitude is not just something we feel, but something we cultivate. It is an intentional practice, a habit of the soul. It is pausing to notice the gifts that surround us, to whisper thanks for the simple joys of the day. It is choosing to see the hand of God in the midst of both laughter and sorrow, knowing that in every moment, He is near.

A grateful heart does not deny the challenges of life, but it faces them with hope. It does not ignore pain, but it looks for purpose even in suffering. It is the heart that, like the young boy in the stable, sees the mess and still believes there must be a pony somewhere.

And so, we begin with gratitude—not as a fleeting emotion, but as a way of life. A way that strengthens us, sustains us, and draws us ever closer to the One who gives us every good and perfect gift.

A Heart Set on Gratitude

Gratitude is a gift, a wellspring of joy, and a source of strength. Yet, it is not a magic remedy that erases hardship or removes every struggle. Life is complex, filled with both mountaintops and valleys where thanksgiving alone does not lighten the weight of suffering. There are seasons of deep sorrow, times when grief or illness presses heavily upon the soul, and moments when faith feels tested beyond measure.

In these times, gratitude is not meant to replace wisdom, nor is it a substitute for the care that our bodies and minds may require. God, in His providence, has given us physicians, counselors, and communities of support for a reason. Seeking help is not a failure of faith but rather an acknowledgment of the many ways He provides for our healing. Still, gratitude has a role to play. It does not dismiss pain, but it does shift our perspective. It reminds us that even in darkness, light is present. Even in suffering, hope remains. Gratitude does not deny reality but helps us see it through a lens of faith—trusting that God is still working, even when we cannot yet see the full picture.

I'm reminded of a deeply personal trial that our family faced in the early years of the new century.

Nancy, my wife, had always been a picture of health and strength—constantly on the go, pouring herself into every task with boundless energy. I often marveled at how she did it all. But then, I began to notice subtle changes. No matter what time of day I returned home, I found her resting, often taking long naps. A quiet concern stirred in my heart. Something wasn't right.

I scheduled an appointment at the clinic in Santa Barbara, California, and our fears were soon confirmed. Nancy was diagnosed with non-Hodgkin's T-cell lymphoma—the same illness that had taken a beloved nephew of ours years before. The weight of those words fell heavily upon us, but even in that moment, we knew we were not alone.

The next year of our lives was marked by relentless trips to Stanford University Medical Center, where Nancy underwent multiple rounds of chemotherapy and other intensive treatments. The road was long, and the battle was fierce. Yet through it all, Nancy's faith never wavered. She clung to the promises of God with unwavering conviction. A minister in our church had prayed over her, speaking a word from the Lord that her healing would be "one for the books." At the time, we had no idea how significant that word would become.

The Key to a Life of Peace and Purpose

Unbeknownst to us, Nancy had been placed in a groundbreaking clinical trial, one that would later be studied by numerous physicians. But what stood out the most during that season was not just the medical advancements—it was Nancy's steadfast heart of gratitude. She lived each day in thanksgiving, believing wholeheartedly in God's faithfulness. Never once did she succumb to despair or disillusionment. Instead, she focused on thanking God for His ultimate healing, even before she saw it come to pass.

One year later, she was declared in remission.

To say that we rejoiced would be an understatement. Our entire family, our church, and even the medical staff who had walked this journey with us stood in awe of God's goodness. The prayers of the faithful had been heard, and Nancy's healing became a testimony of both divine intervention and the power of perseverance.

The beauty of gratitude is that it does not depend on our circumstances. It is not reserved for the easy days, the moments when life unfolds just as we had hoped. Instead, gratitude is an anchor in the storm, a steady force when life feels uncertain.

Cultivating Gratitude

The Apostle Paul, writing from a prison cell, declared,

"I have learned the secret of being content in any and every situation" (Philippians 4:12).

His secret was not in his circumstances but in his perspective—in his unshakable trust in the One who sustains all things.

This is the heart of gratitude: a posture of trust, a refusal to let hardship define our faith, and a daily decision to see God's hand at work even in the midst of trials. And when we embrace this kind of gratitude, we do not merely endure hardship—we overcome it with hearts that are anchored in hope.

And so, gratitude is more than just something we feel; it is something we choose. It is a discipline, a practice, a way of life that draws us ever closer to the heart of God. The psalmist calls us to

"Give thanks to the Lord, for He is good; His love endures forever" (Psalm 107:1).

This is not a command rooted in denial but in truth—His goodness remains, even when life is hard. His love endures, even when we are weary. And gratitude helps us remember.

The benefits of gratitude are not just spiritual; they touch every part of our being. A thankful heart leads to a more peaceful mind, a more resilient spirit, and a greater ability to endure. But gratitude is not merely about what it does for us—it is about who it makes us. It shapes us into people of grace, people of faith, people who walk through life with open hands rather than clenched fists.

This is where we turn from understanding gratitude to living it. It is not enough to know its value; we must embrace it, weaving it into our daily rhythms, letting it become as natural as breathing. It begins with a single choice—to notice, to appreciate, to give thanks. And as we do, we find that gratitude is not just something we practice, it is something that transforms us from the inside out.

As we continue this journey, we will explore how gratitude can be cultivated, not just in moments of abundance, but in the quiet, ordinary, and even difficult seasons of life. For gratitude is not a feeling we wait for, it is a posture we step into, an invitation to walk in joy, no matter what lies ahead.

CHAPTER TWO:

A HEART OF THANKSGIVING IN THE WORD OF GOD

The profound benefits of gratitude, so clearly evident in our own lives, find an even deeper and more lasting foundation in the pages of Scripture. From Genesis to Revelation, the call to thanksgiving resounds—not merely as a suggestion but as a defining mark of a life rooted in faith. Gratitude is not just a fleeting feeling or a polite response to good fortune; it is a spiritual discipline, a posture of the heart that keeps us tethered to God's goodness.

The Key to a Life of Peace and Purpose

The Psalms are filled with this truth, painting a rich picture of gratitude as an act of worship.

"Enter His gates with thanksgiving and His courts with praise; give thanks to Him and praise His name" (Psalm 100:4).

This is not a passive encouragement but an invitation to draw near to God with hearts overflowing in thankfulness. Worship and gratitude are inseparable; one naturally leads to the other. The act of praising God shifts our focus away from our struggles and back to His faithfulness, anchoring our hearts in the reality of His presence.

But gratitude in Scripture is not only a response to blessings, it is also a safeguard against forgetfulness. Deuteronomy 8 warns of the dangers of prosperity without remembrance. The Israelites were repeatedly called to recall how God had sustained them in the wilderness, lest they grow prideful and believe their blessings were of their own making. Gratitude requires intentional remembrance; it is a discipline of the soul that resists complacency and cultivates dependence on God.

Cultivating Gratitude

Perhaps one of the greatest examples of gratitude in hardship is found in the life of David. Despite betrayal, loss, and personal failures, David remained a man after God's own heart, in large part because of his gratitude.

"I will give thanks to you, Lord, with all my heart" (Psalm 9:1).

His thankfulness was not tied to his circumstances—it was rooted in God's unchanging nature. This is the kind of gratitude we are called to cultivate: one that sees beyond the trial and into the faithfulness of God.

Gratitude in the Life of Christ and the Early Church

Jesus Himself modeled a life of thanksgiving. He gave thanks before meals (Matthew 14:19), before performing miracles (John 11:41), and even on the night of His betrayal, when He broke bread with His disciples and gave thanks (Luke 22:19). That moment is particularly striking, knowing the suffering He was about to endure, Jesus still chose gratitude. If the Son of God made thanksgiving a central part of His life, how much more should we?

The Key to a Life of Peace and Purpose

The apostle Paul carried this theme forward, urging believers to

"give thanks in all circumstances, for this is God's will for you in Christ Jesus" (1 Thessalonians 5:18).

Paul's gratitude was not situational, it was deeply rooted in his faith. Writing from prison, he encouraged the Philippians to

"rejoice in the Lord always" (Philippians 4:4)

and to bring their requests before God *"with thanksgiving"* (Philippians 4:6). His letters reveal a man who understood that gratitude is not about denying hardship but about recognizing God's sovereignty in the midst of it.

The example of Job further reinforces this truth. After experiencing unimaginable loss, he still declared,

"The Lord gave, and the Lord has taken away; blessed be the name of the Lord" (Job 1:21).

Cultivating Gratitude

This was not a denial of his pain but a profound statement of trust. Job's suffering was real—his grief deep and his questions many—but his heart remained anchored in the sovereignty of God.

Joseph's life echoes this same theme. Though betrayed by his own brothers, sold into slavery, and unjustly imprisoned, he later saw the divine purpose woven through his trials. He told his brothers,

"You intended to harm me, but God intended it for good" (Genesis 50:20).

His story stands as a testimony that even when life appears chaotic and unfair, God is still at work, orchestrating His plans for our ultimate good.

These stories remind us that gratitude is not about dismissing hardship or pretending suffering does not exist. Rather, it is about trusting that God's purpose is at work within it. We may not always understand why we face trials, but we can rest in the knowledge that nothing is wasted in His hands.

Remaining in a posture of thanksgiving is far easier when we stay rooted in the Word of God, especially during the most difficult seasons of life. Scripture continually reassures us that God is in control, working all things according to His divine will. Romans 8:28 declares this truth: "And we know that all things work together for good to them that love God, to them who are the called according to his purpose."

In moments of hardship, we may be tempted to question, to ask why—but gratitude invites us to shift our focus. Rather than demanding answers, we learn to trust. Instead of fixating on the trial itself, we hold fast to the promise that God is weaving together a greater good, one that will be revealed in His perfect time. Even in the waiting, we can choose to thank Him—not because we understand, but because we trust.

Gratitude as a Spiritual Practice

Scripture presents gratitude as more than a feeling; it is a practice, a discipline, and a way of life. It is a safeguard against pride, a weapon against despair, and a means of deepening our intimacy with God. Living with a grateful heart transforms the way we approach each day. It redirects our focus from what we lack to what we have, from our struggles to God's sufficiency.

True gratitude acknowledges that all good things come from God. It teaches us to see His hand in both the grand and the ordinary—the sunrise, the laughter of a child, the quiet moments of peace. It reminds us that joy is not found in the absence of struggle but in the presence of God.

As we continue this journey, let us move beyond simply understanding gratitude to truly embodying it. Let us make thanksgiving a habit, a prayer, a way of seeing the world. And in doing so, may we discover the abundant life that comes from a heart fully surrendered to God in gratitude.

The biblical foundation for gratitude is both profound and inescapable. It is not a secondary virtue or an optional aspect of faith—it is central to our walk with God. Scripture calls us to thanksgiving not merely as a pleasant practice but as a way of life, a defining characteristic of those who trust in the Lord. From the songs of David to the teachings of Jesus and the exhortations of Paul, gratitude is shown to be a key to spiritual depth, resilience, and a life lived in joyful communion with God.

Gratitude enriches our faith by shifting our focus from our struggles to God's steadfast love. It reminds us that every breath, every provision, every moment of grace is a gift from His hand. When we give thanks, we acknowledge His sovereignty and recognize that His goodness endures beyond our present circumstances. A grateful heart draws us closer to Him, strengthening our trust and deepening our worship.

But gratitude is not just a spiritual ideal, it is a lived reality that shapes our daily existence. When we choose to cultivate thanksgiving, even in hardship, we build resilience. We learn to see through the lens of faith, discovering that even in our trials, God is present and at work. Gratitude transforms not just how we feel, but how we live. It shifts our perspective from scarcity to abundance, from fear to trust, from despair to hope.

The evidence of gratitude's power is both spiritual and practical. Science affirms what Scripture has long declared: a thankful heart is a healthier heart, a peaceful mind, a stronger spirit. It fosters joy, combats anxiety, and opens us to the beauty woven into our everyday lives. By embracing the biblical call to gratitude, we unlock a deeper sense of peace, a richer experience of joy, and a closer walk with God.

Gratitude is more than words spoken in prayer—it is a way of seeing, a way of living, a way of worshiping. As we move forward, may we not merely understand gratitude but embody it. May we cultivate hearts that overflow with thanksgiving, not just in times of blessing, but in all seasons. And in doing so, may we step into the fullness of life that God intends for us—a life marked by faith, resilience, and an ever-deepening awareness of His goodness.

CHAPTER THREE:

THE PRACTICE OF PRESENCE AND GRATITUDE

Cultivating genuine gratitude is not a passive experience; it is an intentional practice that requires our full attention and commitment. It asks us to quiet the restless noise of our thoughts, to step away from the weight of yesterday's regrets and tomorrow's uncertainties, and to fully embrace the gift of the present moment. This is where gratitude thrives—not in a hurried mind, but in a heart that is attuned to the blessings of now.

The Key to a Life of Peace and Purpose

When our thoughts are consumed with what was or what might be, we miss the beauty of what is. Rumination over past mistakes and anxieties about the future can keep us from recognizing the grace woven into our daily lives. We can be so caught up in our own inner storms that we fail to notice the simple, sacred gifts that God places before us—a warm meal, the laughter of a loved one, the way the morning light filters through the trees. These moments are rich with opportunities for gratitude, but too often, they go unnoticed.

This is where the practice of mindfulness becomes a powerful tool for deepening our gratitude. At its core, mindfulness is the simple yet profound discipline of being fully present—of noticing without distraction, of appreciating without rushing past. In a faith-based perspective, mindfulness is not merely a mental exercise; it is a way of tuning our hearts to the nearness of God. It is the practice of recognizing His hand in the details of our lives, allowing us to respond with gratitude for even the smallest of blessings.

Mindfulness as a Path to Gratitude

The Bible speaks often of being still before the Lord, of meditating on His goodness, and of seeking Him in the quiet places of our hearts.

"Be still, and know that I am God" (Psalm 46:10)

is not merely a call to silence but an invitation to presence—an awareness that makes space for gratitude. When we intentionally focus on the present moment, we become more receptive to the many ways God is providing for us, guiding us, and surrounding us with His love.

Mindfulness, in the biblical sense, is not an emptying of the mind but a filling—an intentional turning of our thoughts toward God, His presence, and His works. It is the practice of slowing down, of quieting the noise of life long enough to recognize His hand in the everyday moments. This awareness cultivates gratitude, allowing us to see God's provision in the smallest details.

This mindfulness can be nurtured through simple, practical exercises. Take a moment during the day to step away from distractions, find a quiet place, and center your heart on God's presence. As you walk outdoors, resist the urge to rush—pause to fully experience the world around you. Notice the vibrant colors, the gentle rustling of leaves, the warmth of the sun on your face. Feel the coolness of a breeze, listen to birdsong, or take in the sweet fragrance of blooming flowers. And as you do, whisper a prayer of thanks to God for His creation, for the beauty He has woven into every moment.

The lyrics of George Strait's song, "I Saw God Today," capture this very sentiment:

Just walked down the street to the coffee shop
Had to take a break
I've been by her side for 18 hours straight
Saw a flower growing in the middle of the
sidewalk
Pushing up through the concrete
Like it was planted right there for me to see
The flashing lights, the honking horn
All seem to fade away
In the shadow of the hospital at 5:08
I saw God today

How often do we rush through life without noticing Him? His fingerprints are everywhere—in the kindness of a stranger, the laughter of a child, the unexpected moment of peace amid chaos. When we slow down and truly see, we realize that God has been there all along, weaving His grace into our daily experiences. If that doesn't inspire gratitude, what possibly could?

Mindfulness is not about forcing ourselves to never be distracted, but rather about gently bringing our hearts back—again and again—to the present, to gratitude, and to God. It is a spiritual discipline, a practice of noticing and naming His blessings, of training our hearts to recognize His presence in all things. And as we do, we find that gratitude is no longer something we practice only in prayer but something that permeates every moment of our lives.

The Grateful Heart

When we cultivate presence, gratitude naturally follows. Instead of focusing on what we lack, we begin to see the abundance of what we have. Instead of allowing fear to dictate our thoughts, we allow thanksgiving to shape them.

A grateful heart does not wait for perfect circumstances to rejoice—it finds joy in the ordinary, in

The Key to a Life of Peace and Purpose

the overlooked, in the simple and sacred moments of life. It recognizes that each day is a gift, each breath a blessing, each moment an opportunity to see God at work.

This shift is not only spiritual but transformative to our well-being. As gratitude takes root, it changes our outlook, our relationships, and our sense of peace. Instead of allowing life to rush past us, we begin to live fully aware of God's goodness, receptive to His grace, and eager to give thanks.

But this is a journey, not a destination. There will be days when we are distracted, when worry creeps in, when gratitude feels distant. In those moments, we do not give up. Instead, we return to the practice of presence, reminding ourselves that God is here, that His blessings abound, and that a thankful heart is always within reach.

Because in the end, gratitude is not something we find, it is something we choose. And when we choose it, we step into the fullness of the life God has always intended for us: a life of peace, of joy, and of deep and abiding thanksgiving.

The Practice of Gratitude in Daily Life

Embarking on the journey of gratitude, especially in the beginning, can feel like standing at the foot of a great mountain. With so much to process each day—moments of joy and hardship, triumph and trial—it can feel overwhelming to sift through the noise and discern the blessings woven into our daily lives. But gratitude is not about grand gestures or extraordinary events. Its beauty lies in its simplicity, in the quiet recognition of the good that surrounds us, no matter how small. It is a posture of the heart, a habit we cultivate with intention and patience.

One of the most effective ways to develop this habit is through the practice of gratitude journaling. A gratitude journal serves as a personal record of blessings—a testament to the goodness of God, even in the midst of life's uncertainties. This practice does not require eloquence or long reflections; it simply invites consistency. A few sentences each day, a handful of moments noted with thanksgiving, can transform the way we see the world. We'll discuss this in more detail in Chapter eight.

Cultivating Gratitude

To help cultivate a lifestyle of gratitude, consider using simple prompts during your daily devotional time. These quiet moments with the Lord are opportunities not only to offer petitions or seek wisdom, but to reflect upon the blessings that might have otherwise slipped past unnoticed. Life moves fast, and if we're not intentional, it's easy to miss the fingerprints of God woven into the fabric of our day.

I'll be honest—I'm a task-oriented person. When I'm focused on a project, I tend to tune out everything around me. Someone could walk by and drop off a package I was supposed to retrieve, sparing me the trouble, and I may not even notice the thoughtful act, let alone say thank you. If I can overlook kindness from those around me, how much more do I risk missing the unceasing goodness of God extended toward me day after day?

That's why it's so helpful to pause, even for just a few minutes, and ask ourselves some guiding questions. These prompts invite our hearts to slow down, reflect, and recognize the hand of God at work in the everyday.

What three things am I grateful for today?
This gentle question shifts our focus from what's lacking to what's already present. The blessings don't have to be grand—a warm conversation, a shared laugh, a safe drive home. Gratitude grows when we notice the small things.

What small act of kindness did I experience or witness?
When we choose to notice kindness, we amplify it. A stranger's smile, a coworker's help, or a child's hug becomes more than a passing moment—it becomes a reminder that goodness still surrounds us.

What am I grateful for about my health?
Health is often overlooked until it is compromised. Even on difficult days, there is usually something to give thanks for—the ability to breathe deeply, to walk without pain, to open our eyes and see the light of a new day.

What aspect of my surroundings am I grateful for?
Whether it's the quiet of the morning, the warmth

of your home, the way sunlight pours across the floor, or the sound of your favorite worship song—creation itself testifies to God's provision. Noticing the beauty around us draws our hearts into worship.

What relationships am I thankful for?
People are God's gift to us. A friend who listens. A spouse who prays. A child who brings laughter. A stranger who held a door. Naming these people before God reminds us that love is a gift worth treasuring. This one prompt can help lead us into intercessory prayer on another's behalf.

The goal of these prompts isn't to fill a page—it's to fill the heart. Reflection is what transforms a fleeting moment into a holy one. When we slow down long enough to really see, gratitude begins to take root.

Personally, I begin every conversation with God by saying, *"Lord, I thank You for Your love, Your mercy, and Your grace. I acknowledge You as the Lord of my life."* Those simple words awaken something in my spirit. They shift my posture and center my heart. Often, as soon as I speak them, the Holy Spirit begins to remind me of the goodness God has shown me—just in the past few days, or even hours. His faithfulness rushes in like a flood.

You may wonder, *why begin every prayer this way?* The answer is simple: without the relentless pursuit of God's mercy and the reckless grace that found me in the depths of my failure, I would not be who I am today. I *could not* be where I am today.

There's a song, *"God is in This Story"* by Katy Nicole that captures my heart perfectly:

There's torn up pages in this book
Words that tell me I'm no good
Chapters that defined me for so long
But the hands of grace and endless love
Dusted off and picked me up
Told my heart that hope is never gone
... God is in this story
God is in the details
Even in the broken parts
He holds my heart, He never fails
When I'm at my weakest
I will trust in Jesus
Always in the highs and lows
The One who goes before me

The Key to a Life of Peace and Purpose

God is in this story so yes, I begin every prayer with thanksgiving—for His love that never gives up, His mercy that never runs dry, and His grace, the most undeserved and beautiful gift ever given to mankind. Gratitude isn't just something I practice. It's the heartbeat of my walk with the Lord. And it's from that place of thanksgiving that everything else in my life now flows.

CHAPTER FOUR:

EXPRESSING
GRATITUDE TO OTHERS

Gratitude is not meant to remain private; it is meant to be shared. When we express thankfulness to others, we strengthen relationships, deepen our appreciation, and extend the blessings we have received. A sincere "thank you" has the power to brighten someone's day, but it does more than that—it fosters a culture of gratitude, a way of life where kindness is noticed, valued, and multiplied.

There are countless ways to share gratitude, each carrying its own significance. Sometimes, it is as simple as speaking a word of thanks. A heartfelt expression of appreciation, whether in a conversation or a brief message, can create warmth and connection, reminding both the giver and the receiver of the goodness that exists between them.

At other times, gratitude is best expressed in writing. A handwritten note, though small, carries a special weight. In a world of hurried texts and emails, taking the time to put thankfulness into words shows intentionality and care. A simple letter of appreciation, whether to a friend, a mentor, or even a stranger who has made a difference, can leave a lasting impact that goes beyond the moment.

Beyond words, gratitude is also revealed through action. An act of service—a helping hand, an encouraging presence, or a quiet gesture of support—can speak volumes. Sometimes, gratitude looks like preparing a meal for a weary friend, running an errand for a loved one, or offering a listening ear to someone who needs to be heard. These acts, no matter how small, show appreciation in ways that words alone cannot fully convey.

When we take the time to express gratitude sincerely, we bless others, but we also reinforce our own gratitude. The simple act of recognizing and voicing appreciation shifts our focus toward the good, reminding us of the abundance already present in our lives. And as gratitude is shared, it creates a ripple effect—one expression inspiring another, one heart lifting another—until the blessings extend far beyond what we could have imagined.

Gratitude for Kingdom-Minded Givers

When we speak of expressing gratitude to others, we dare not forget the Kingdom minded givers that support the most important work ever delegated to man; that of making disciples of all men, as commanded by Jesus

One of the most humbling and beautiful expressions of gratitude we can preform in ministry is the recognition of those who give—not for recognition or reward—but out of obedience, compassion, and Kingdom vision. As someone privileged to serve in a ministry supported solely by donors, I have come to see just how sacred these acts of generosity truly are.

Behind every gift, there is a story. A decision. A sacrifice. Whether large or small, each donation is an expression of faith, seeds sown into the soil of eternal impact. These faithful supporters may never meet the people whose lives are changed, they may never see the full fruit of their giving, but they give anyway. Why? Because they believe in the work of God. They believe in the power of the Gospel. And they believe that their resources—when surrendered to God—can accomplish more than they ever imagined.

As recipients of that generosity, we have a holy responsibility—not only to steward those gifts wisely but also to express heartfelt gratitude. A handwritten note, a sincere prayer lifted on their behalf, a personal phone call, or even a story shared about the lives being transformed—all are meaningful ways to say, *"Thank you for being a part of what God is doing."*

Paul modeled this beautifully in his letters to the churches. In Philippians 1:3–5, he writes,

"I thank my God every time I remember you. In all my prayers for all of you, I always pray with joy because of your partnership in the gospel from the first day until now."

That is the heart we must carry—a spirit of gratitude for every person who stands beside us in Kingdom work.

Donors are more than contributors; they are partners in the harvest. Their faith fuels the ministry. Their generosity sends missionaries, feeds the hungry, supports programs, and builds places where people can encounter Christ. We must never take their sacrifice for granted.

To every Kingdom-minded giver reading these words: thank you. You are seen by God. Your gift matters. Your faith is not in vain. And your reward—though not always visible here on earth—is being stored up in heaven where moth and rust cannot destroy. You are part of every changed life, every restored heart, every soul won for Christ.

And from the bottom of my heart, Thank You!

Gratitude in the Workplace

The principles of gratitude, so powerfully demonstrated in personal relationships, extend seamlessly into the professional sphere. Cultivating gratitude at work isn't merely a feel-good exercise; it's a strategic approach to fostering a more positive, productive, and fulfilling work environment. A

The Key to a Life of Peace and Purpose

grateful mindset can significantly impact individual well-being and contribute to a more harmonious and effective team dynamic. This isn't about blind positivity or ignoring legitimate workplace challenges. It's about consciously shifting perspective to acknowledge and appreciate the positive aspects of our work experiences, even amidst demanding circumstances.

One of the most fundamental strategies is expressing gratitude to colleagues. This isn't limited to grand gestures; small acts of appreciation can have a profound impact. A simple "thank you" for assistance on a project, acknowledgment of a colleague's expertise, or a compliment on their work ethic can significantly boost morale and strengthen working relationships. Consider actively seeking opportunities to express appreciation for the contributions of others. Did a colleague go the extra mile to meet a deadline? Did someone offer valuable insight during a challenging meeting? Take a moment to verbally express your gratitude. A brief email or a handwritten note can also be powerfully effective, especially in situations where face-to-face interaction may be limited.

Cultivating Gratitude

The impact extends beyond immediate colleagues. Expressing gratitude to supervisors fosters a more positive and collaborative work environment. Acknowledging a manager's support, guidance, or trust can strengthen your professional bond and enhance your working relationship. Avoid assuming that your supervisors are simply fulfilling their duties; actively appreciate their contributions and the efforts they make to support their teams. This can be conveyed through a concise email expressing your appreciation for a specific action or through a more formal conversation highlighting their positive influence on your professional growth. Such gestures build mutual respect and create a more open and communicative work environment.

Gratitude extends to clients as well. Expressing sincere appreciation for their business, their trust, or their feedback, regardless of its nature, can significantly impact your working relationship. A simple "thank you" for their continued patronage, a thoughtful follow-up email after a project is completed, or a proactive response to feedback, positive or negative, demonstrates professionalism and a genuine interest in nurturing the client relationship. This practice enhances client loyalty, fosters positive word-of-mouth referrals, and contributes to a more positive and sustainable working environment.

Beyond verbal expressions, consider incorporating other strategies for cultivating gratitude in the workplace. Keeping a gratitude journal focused specifically on work-related experiences can be profoundly beneficial. Each evening, take a few minutes to reflect on the positive aspects of your workday. Did you successfully complete a challenging task? Did you learn something new? Did you collaborate effectively with a colleague? Documenting these positive experiences reinforces a grateful perspective and helps to counteract any negative feelings that may have accumulated throughout the day.

Furthermore, incorporating mindfulness practices into your workday can enhance your ability to appreciate the positive aspects of your work. Even short periods of mindful meditation can help to shift your perspective, allowing you to focus on the present moment and appreciate the opportunities and accomplishments that often go unnoticed in the midst of a busy schedule. Mindful breathing exercises, practiced throughout the workday, can reduce stress and enhance your ability to approach tasks with a more positive and appreciative attitude.

Another effective strategy is to actively seek opportunities to help others. Offering support to colleagues, taking on additional responsibilities, or simply offering a helping hand can foster a more collaborative and appreciative work environment. When we assist others, we not only contribute to a more positive work environment, but we also experience a sense of accomplishment and purpose, further enhancing our overall sense of gratitude. This reciprocal relationship between offering assistance and feeling grateful strengthens team cohesion and fosters a spirit of mutual support.

Creating a gratitude-focused workplace culture requires a concerted effort from all levels. Leadership can play a crucial role by actively modeling gratitude, publicly acknowledging employee contributions, and fostering a culture of appreciation. This may involve incorporating regular team meetings that specifically focus on celebrating achievements and expressing gratitude for each member's contribution. Alternatively, leadership could institute a peer-to-peer recognition program, where employees can nominate colleagues for outstanding contributions, reinforcing the importance of mutual appreciation within the team.

In addition to leadership initiatives, team-building exercises that incorporate gratitude practices can significantly enhance workplace morale and cooperation. This could involve a simple exercise where each team member shares one thing they appreciate about another member, or a more extensive activity that encourages reflection on shared achievements and expressions of gratitude for mutual support. The purpose is to shift focus to the positive aspects of working together, building camaraderie and fostering stronger collaborative bonds within the team. These collective expressions of gratitude build a strong foundation for a supportive work environment.

The benefits of cultivating gratitude at work extend far beyond improved morale. Research consistently demonstrates a strong correlation between gratitude and increased productivity. A grateful mindset enhances focus, reduces stress, and improves overall job satisfaction, leading to increased efficiency and higher quality of work. This ultimately contributes to the success of the organization as a whole. By promoting a culture of gratitude, organizations create a more sustainable, productive, and ultimately, more successful workplace. It is an investment in both individual and collective well-being, fostering an environment where employees feel valued, appreciated, and motivated to achieve their full potential.

Furthermore, a workplace imbued with gratitude is more resilient to stress and challenges. When individuals cultivate a sense of appreciation for their work, their colleagues, and their accomplishments, they are better equipped to navigate stressful situations and overcome obstacles. This resilience translates into greater adaptability, improved problem-solving skills, and a greater capacity to maintain a positive outlook even in challenging circumstances. This resilience is a critical asset in today's dynamic and often unpredictable work environment.

Finally, it is essential to emphasize that cultivating gratitude in the workplace is an ongoing process, not a quick fix. It requires consistent effort, mindful practice, and a commitment to actively seeking and expressing appreciation. It's a journey of cultivating a positive perspective, focusing on the good, and recognizing the value of both individual and collective contributions. The rewards, however, are substantial, creating a more fulfilling, productive, and resilient work environment for everyone involved. The transformation is not just about individual happiness; it is about creating a more positive, collaborative, and ultimately successful organization. It's a testament to the power of a grateful heart to shape a better world, starting with our workspaces.

Gratitude as a Lifelong Practice

Developing a grateful heart is not a one-time effort; it is a lifelong journey. It is an ongoing decision to see through the lens of abundance rather than scarcity, to focus on blessings rather than burdens, to acknowledge God's goodness in every season.

This is not always easy. There will be days when gratitude feels elusive, when worries press in, when the world seems heavy. But even in those moments, there is something to be thankful for—the breath in our lungs, the nearness of God, the hope that is never lost.

Each small step—each journal entry, each moment of mindful appreciation, each word of thanks—brings us deeper into the practice of gratitude. And as this practice becomes a way of life, we will find that joy, peace, and contentment naturally follow.

Because gratitude is not about having more; it is about seeing more. It is not about waiting for blessings; it is about recognizing the ones that are already here. And when we choose to live with grateful hearts, we step into a life of deeper faith, richer relationships, and a profound awareness of God's presence in all things.

CHAPTER FIVE:

THE TRANSFORMATIVE POWER OF A GRATEFUL HEART

The transformative power of a grateful heart is undeniable. When we intentionally cultivate gratitude, it begins to change how we see the world, how we experience our faith, and how we respond to both joy and hardship. It softens our hearts, steadies our spirits, and opens our eyes to the beauty woven into the everyday. And one of the most powerful tools in this sacred journey is the written word.

The Key to a Life of Peace and Purpose

When life feels chaotic or burdens heavy the soul, journaling allows you to pause and listen to what's stirring inside. By putting your thoughts on paper, you gain clarity. The jumbled feelings that cloud your mind begin to take shape. Patterns emerge. Triggers are exposed. And most importantly, truths come into focus—truths about God's goodness, about His nearness, and about His faithfulness to walk beside you through every valley.

It's not always easy. Sometimes, the first words scratched into a journal are angry, confused, or exhausted. But here's the beauty: God isn't afraid of those words. In fact, He welcomes them. The Psalms are full of David's raw honesty—cries for help, declarations of fear, and at times, deep lament. And yet, David nearly always ends in gratitude.

Why? Because when we bring our whole selves before God, even through ink on a page, He meets us there. Journaling becomes a mirror—not just reflecting what is broken, but also revealing where God is building something new.

A gratitude journal becomes far more than just a collection of passing thoughts. Over time, it transforms into a sacred space—a personal sanctuary where we pause to record our blessings, acknowledge God's hand in our lives, and foster a deeper awareness of His constant goodness. The act of writing slows the mind's racing thoughts, gently drawing us into the present moment. In that stillness, we begin to fully appreciate the grace that quietly surrounds us.

But journaling is not simply about listing blessings; it is about engaging the heart. It is an invitation to reflect, to remember, to shift our perspective, and to allow gratitude to take root deep within our spirits. With consistency, this practice begins to retrain our minds—leading us away from the exhausting posture of scarcity and into a life marked by contentment and appreciation. Gratitude no longer becomes something reserved for the extraordinary. Instead, it reveals itself in the seemingly ordinary—a warm cup of coffee on a chilly morning, a kind word offered at just the right time, or the steady presence of a faithful friend.

To make gratitude journaling meaningful and enriching spiritual practice, intentionality is essential. Writing with specificity brings our thanksgiving to life. A general statement like, *"I'm grateful for my family,"* becomes far more impactful when tied to a specific moment: *"Tonight, I am grateful for the laughter around the dinner table, the stories shared, and the simple joy of being together."* The more vividly we describe our gratitude, the more deeply it impresses upon our hearts.

Beyond naming what we're thankful for, our gratitude deepens when we reflect on *why.* If we're thankful for a friend, what have they done that blessed us? If we're grateful for a lesson, how has it changed us? A journal entry might say, *"Today, I am grateful for the work I do, not only because it provides for my family, but because of the unexpected kindness of a coworker who encouraged me in a difficult moment. It reminded me that I am not alone."* When we connect gratitude to meaning, it becomes more than an emotion—it becomes a foundation of faith.

Faith plays a vital role in this process. Gratitude journaling can become an act of worship when we invite scripture and prayer into the practice. By recording verses that speak of God's faithfulness, documenting answered prayers, or simply expressing thanks for His daily presence, our journals become altars of remembrance. An entry might read, *"I read Psalm 23 today, and was reminded again that the*

Cultivating Gratitude

Lord is my Shepherd—I have all that I need. His presence comforts me, even in uncertainty." Or perhaps, *"I'm thankful for the roof over my head, the food on my table, and the warmth of my home—daily reminders that God is faithful."*

Perhaps the most transformative expression of gratitude comes when we find it in seasons of hardship. Gratitude doesn't erase pain, but it reframes it. It allows us to search for signs of God's presence even in our sorrow. An entry written during a season of waiting might say, *"Though the answers haven't come yet, I'm thankful for the strength God is building in me. I'm learning to trust Him more fully, and that is a gift I didn't expect."* Gratitude in suffering becomes an anchor—it holds us steady and draws us deeper into the heart of God.

On days when inspiration is harder to find, simple prompts can gently guide our reflections. Thoughtful questions like, *"How did I see God's grace today?"* or *"What spiritual lesson am I thankful for?"* or *"What is one way I can express gratitude to God today?"* help us tune our hearts to the rhythms of His goodness. These prompts don't demand long answers—only a willing heart.

The Key to a Life of Peace and Purpose

One of the most beautiful aspects of journaling is the ability to look back. Flipping through pages of past entries, we begin to see the quiet thread of God's faithfulness woven through the tapestry of our lives. We recall moments of answered prayer, seasons of growth, and blessings we may have forgotten. A gratitude journal becomes a living testimony—proof of a God who provides, who sustains, who never leaves.

This truth came home in a powerful way after my mother's passing. As my siblings and I gathered at her home, we were handed her prayer journal. It was filled with the petitions she had laid before the Lord over the years, each one written with faith, and each one wrapped in gratitude. She had not only made her requests known to God; she had also given thanks, even before the answers came.

And there, woven throughout the pages, were our names. Prayers for us. Thanksgiving for us. Trust that God would guide, protect, restore, and bless us. Some of those prayers changed the course of our lives—divinely redirected paths we hadn't even realized were answers to her petitions. Holding that journal, reading her words, we understood the power of a life lived in gratitude. She had trusted God fully, and that trust was etched on every page. Her journal became her legacy.

There is no one right way to journal. For some, structured bullet points work best. For others, it may be free-flowing thoughts, poetry, sketches, or letters written to God. What matters is that the practice resonates with your heart and allows gratitude to find its voice.

When we begin to live from this place, gratitude becomes more than a feeling. It becomes a way of seeing, a way of being, a way of worshiping. It shapes our perspective, softens our hearts, and deepens our walk with the Lord.

This journey of gratitude isn't about perfection or producing profound words. It's about daily choosing to notice, to appreciate, and to respond with thanksgiving. In doing so, we not only recognize the gifts—we honor the Giver.

Let gratitude be more than something you feel. Let it be something you live.

CHAPTER SIX:

THE PRACTICE OF MINDFUL REFLECTION IN GRATITUDE

Mindful reflection is more than a fleeting acknowledgment of blessings; it is an intentional act of engaging the heart and spirit in gratitude. It invites us to slow down, quiet the restless distractions of our minds, and recognize the subtle yet profound ways God's goodness surrounds us. In a world that often urges us to rush ahead, to dwell on what is missing, or to worry about what's next, mindful reflection reorients us—it calls us back to the present, to a posture of appreciation, and to an awareness of God's hand in every moment.

The Psalms echo this truth, urging us to;

"Be still, and know that I am God" (Psalm 46:10).

Stillness allows gratitude to take root. It is in these quiet moments that we can truly reflect, acknowledge, and respond to the countless ways God's presence fills our lives. This is not a passive process but an active, transformative practice that reshapes our hearts and minds to see His blessings more clearly.

I came to understand the power of silence before God in a deeply personal way shortly after being released from federal prison in 2019. My middle son, Ben, invited me to attend a men's retreat, and though I was hesitant, I accepted. On the first day, we were challenged to take a vow of silence for eight hours, to find a place of solitude, and to simply meditate before God. At first, the thought of sitting in silence seemed daunting. My mind was filled with the weight of my past, the uncertainty of my future, and the deep wounds I had carried for so long.

But as the hours passed, something profound happened. In the stillness, God met me in a way I had never experienced before. His presence was undeniable. It was in that sacred quiet that He restored me completely, washing over me with a grace so tangible that it became more real than at any other time in my life. In that silence, I found healing. In that stillness, I encountered the depth of His love.

Looking back, I realize that had I not taken that time to be still before Him, I would not be sitting here today, writing these words with a heart overflowing with gratitude. Before that moment, the weight of my past had always seemed too great, the regret too heavy. But when I finally pushed aside the pain of yesterday and placed Him first in my thoughts, He spoke a truth into my heart that I will forever hold dear: *I was His.* No matter where I had been, no matter what I had done, I belonged to Him.

Now, at the ministry where I serve, I often make a joke with those around me—I tell them, *"I am God's favorite kid."* We laugh about it, but deep down, that's exactly how I feel. Not because I am more deserving or because I have done anything to earn it, but because I have tasted the depths of His grace. And when you've encountered the kind of love that restores and redeems, it's impossible not to walk in gratitude.

The Power of Guided Reflection and Contemplation

One way to cultivate this deep sense of gratitude is through guided meditation—creating space in our day to intentionally reflect on God's blessings. This is not about emptying the mind but about focusing it, directing our thoughts toward thanksgiving and awareness.

Begin by finding a quiet space, perhaps in a comfortable chair, by a window, or in nature. Close your eyes and take a deep breath, allowing the noise of the day to settle. As you inhale, acknowledge God's presence; as you exhale, release any stress or distractions that weigh on your heart.

Then, gently bring to mind one blessing—just one. Instead of rushing through a mental list, linger on this gift. If it is the warmth of the sun, feel its presence on your skin. If it is a loved one's kindness, recall their voice, their words, their love in action. If it is the ability to walk, breathe, or see, allow yourself to recognize the miracle of your own body functioning in ways you often take for granted.

As you dwell on this blessing, offer a simple prayer of gratitude. I promise you; He'll meet you where you are. You'll be able to feel the tangible presence of the Holy Spirit as He embraces your prayers of thanksgiving.

By practicing this slow, mindful reflection, gratitude moves beyond mere thought—it becomes something you experience, something that sinks into your soul and reshapes how you see the world.

The Role of Contemplative Prayer in Gratitude

Gratitude and prayer are inseparable. When we practice mindful reflection, it is natural for our hearts to turn toward conversation with God—not as a rigid or formal exercise, but as a simple and honest exchange of thanksgiving.

Contemplative prayer offers a powerful way to deepen gratitude. Unlike structured prayers that focus on requests or petitions, contemplative prayer is a time of simply resting in God's presence, allowing gratitude to overflow from a heart that is fully aware of His goodness. In these quiet moments, when we cease striving and simply dwell in the nearness of God, our souls become more attuned to

The Key to a Life of Peace and Purpose

His faithfulness. Gratitude no longer feels like something we must force ourselves to practice—it becomes a natural response to the overwhelming presence of His love.

One of the ways I prepare my heart for prayer is by listening to worship music. As soon as I turn on my playlist, my spirit shifts into an attitude of thanksgiving. The lyrics remind me of God's promises, His provision, and His unchanging nature. Before I even say a word in prayer, I find myself filled with gratitude, simply because I have taken the time to soak in the truth of who He is.

Beyond contemplative prayer, worship music has a way of stirring spontaneous praise and thanksgiving to God. It's not unusual for me to be driving down the road, listening to my playlist, when suddenly, I'm overcome with gratitude. Without even realizing it, I begin to lift my voice in praise, thanking God for His goodness in my life. In these moments, I am reminded that worship is not confined to a church building or a designated prayer time—it is woven into the fabric of everyday life. Whether in stillness or in song, gratitude is always within reach, waiting to be awakened by the awareness of His presence

When you pray, enter into prayer with no agenda other than to express thanks. Speak freely, not rushing through a list, but allowing each word to come from a place of sincerity.

Allow moments of silence to follow your words. Let God's presence fill those pauses, and rest in the awareness of His love. This stillness, this quiet communion, becomes a space where gratitude deepens, where our hearts align with His, and where thanksgiving becomes a way of drawing nearer to Him.

Simple Daily Practices for Mindful Gratitude

Gratitude is not confined to structured times of prayer and meditation; it can be woven seamlessly into the rhythm of daily life through small, intentional moments of reflection. These simple practices, when embraced consistently, have the power to transform the way we perceive and experience the world around us.

One of the most effective ways to cultivate gratitude is by pausing throughout the day to acknowledge even the simplest blessings. These "mindful moments" do not require grand gestures or extensive effort—only an intentional awareness of God's goodness. Imagine starting your morning with a cup of coffee, but rather than drinking it in a hurried rush, you take a moment to savor its warmth, breathe in its aroma, and silently thank God for the provision of food and drink. Or perhaps, in the middle of a busy afternoon, you hear the joyful laughter of a child. Instead of letting the sound fade into the background, you pause to fully take it in, acknowledging the simple joy it brings. Even stepping outside for a brief moment can become an act of worship—feeling the cool breeze, gazing at the sky, and whispering a prayer of thanks for the beauty of creation. These small acts of awareness, practiced day after day, gently reshape the heart toward a posture of greater gratitude.

At the ministry where I now serve, I am privileged to teach on occasion. Most of my instruction is directed toward young people dedicated to serving Christ through Servant Leadership. Recently, I had the opportunity to teach a group called the "Posties," young men and women who have committed themselves to volunteering at our camp while studying God's Word for nine months. The lesson I shared with them that day was on this very subject—*Cultivating Gratitude.*

For some reason, the message resonated deeply with Claire, one of the young women serving here. From that day forward, she has made it a personal mission to approach the staff members daily with a simple yet profound question: *"What are you grateful for today?"*

At first, it may have seemed like just a friendly inquiry, but over time, this simple question has become a powerful exercise in mindfulness and thanksgiving. Each day, when staff members are approached, they take a moment to pause, contemplate, and provide an answer. In doing so, they become more aware of the blessings in their lives, no matter how big or small. The beauty of Claire's practice is that it not only enriches those who respond but also blesses her in return. She witnesses firsthand how gratitude lifts the spirits of those around her, drawing their focus back to God's goodness.

Her daily question has become more than a habit—it is now a ministry in itself. Through her simple act of asking, *"What are you grateful for today?"* she has cultivated a culture of thanksgiving,

The Key to a Life of Peace and Purpose

one small conversation at a time. And in those brief moments of reflection, gratitude takes root, transforming hearts and turning everyday encounters into acts of worship.

Claire's story is a testament to how a simple question can transform the way we see the world. When gratitude feels distant or difficult to grasp, intentional reflection can serve as a guide, drawing the mind back to the evidence of God's presence. Just as Claire's daily question", *What are you grateful for today?"*, invited others to pause and recognize their blessings, personal reflection prompts can help shift our focus from what is lacking to what is already present.

Asking ourselves, *"What is one way God showed His love for me today?"* or *"What moment of peace or joy did I experience?"* encourages us to notice the quiet yet powerful ways God moves in our lives. Even in the midst of hardship, prompts like, *"Who has shown me kindness today, and how can I express gratitude for them?"* or *"How have I seen God's hand at work this week?"* remind us that blessings abound, even if they are not immediately visible.

Cultivating Gratitude

Just as Claire's question caused those around her to pause and reflect, speaking these reflections aloud or writing them down deepens their impact. What might have been a fleeting moment of appreciation becomes a deeply ingrained awareness of God's goodness. The more we practice gratitude, the more it becomes second nature—an attitude that shapes our perspective and leads us into deeper communion with Him.

Perhaps one of the greatest challenges in cultivating gratitude is learning to find it within hardships. The Apostle Paul's words in 1 Thessalonians 5:18 urge us to "give thanks in all circumstances." This does not mean we are expected to be grateful for suffering itself, but rather, we are invited to discover gratitude even within it. In the midst of pain, loss, or uncertainty, there is always something to hold onto—the lessons being learned, the strength being developed, the love and support of those around us, and most importantly, the sustaining presence of God. By shifting our perspective from asking "Why is this happening?" to "What can I learn from this?" we begin to see difficulties through a different lens, one that reveals God's faithfulness even in the midst of trials.

The Key to a Life of Peace and Purpose

Gratitude is not about ignoring reality or pretending that hardships do not exist. It is about choosing to see the evidence of grace woven throughout every season of life. When we cultivate an awareness of His presence, both in the joys and in the struggles, we come to understand that gratitude is not just something we practice, it becomes a way of living.

Gratitude as a Journey of Faith

Practicing gratitude through mindful reflection is not about forcing ourselves to feel thankful at all times. It is about creating space in our lives to recognize God's goodness, to acknowledge His hand in the details, and to respond with a heart that overflows in thanksgiving.

This journey takes patience. Some days, gratitude comes easily; other days, it feels distant. But as we continue to pause, to reflect, and to give thanks, we will find that gratitude becomes not just something we do, but something we *become*. It will shape our thoughts, our words, our prayers, and our faith.

In time, we will see that gratitude is not only for the moments of blessing—it is a constant companion, a source of strength, and a way of walking ever closer with God.

As we embrace this journey, let us be encouraged by the words of Colossians 3:17:

"And whatever you do, whether in word or deed, do it all in the name of the Lord Jesus, giving thanks to God the Father through Him."

Let us choose to live in gratitude—not just as a fleeting emotion, but as a way of life, a reflection of faith, and a response to the unending goodness of our Creator.

CHAPTER SEVEN: THE SACRED UNION OF GRATITUDE AND PRAYER

Gratitude is more than a fleeting feeling—it is a discipline, a way of seeing the world through the lens of God's abundant grace. Prayer, in its purest form, is a divine conversation, an invitation to communion with the One who knows our hearts. When these two practices intertwine, something powerful happens: prayer deepens our gratitude, and gratitude transforms our prayers. Together, they create a wellspring of faith, trust, and joy.

Paul's exhortation in *Philippians 4:6-7* speaks directly to this truth:

The Key to a Life of Peace and Purpose

"Do not be anxious about anything, but in every situation, by prayer and petition, with thanksgiving, present your requests to God. And the peace of God, which transcends all understanding, will guard your hearts and your minds in Christ Jesus."

Here, thanksgiving is not an afterthought but a central part of prayer—one that leads directly to peace.

Beginning Prayer with Thanksgiving

One of the simplest yet most profound ways to integrate gratitude into prayer is by beginning each prayer with thanksgiving. Before presenting any petitions or concerns, take a moment to acknowledge God's goodness. Reflect on the ways He has provided, sustained, and guided you.

This simple shift in focus creates a spirit of openness, reminding us that we are approaching a God who is already working for our good.

The Practice of Contemplative Prayer in Gratitude

Contemplative prayer offers us a sacred invitation—not to speak, not to strive, but simply to be. It is a quiet returning to God's presence, a stilling of the soul, and a resting of the heart in the awareness that we are deeply loved. And in that stillness, something beautiful begins to rise: gratitude, not forced or fabricated, but born naturally out of being with Him.

Contemplative prayer requires no words at all. It is not about asking or explaining. It is about abiding. It is the spiritual posture of Mary, who sat at the feet of Jesus and simply listened, while Martha busied herself with many things. In contemplative prayer, we bring no agenda—only our longing to dwell with the One who formed us, redeemed us, and calls us His own.

In a world that constantly demands our attention, contemplative prayer slows us down. It invites us to push aside distraction, to let go of worry, and to step into the quiet where God's voice is often the clearest. And there, in the stillness, gratitude begins to bloom. Not a gratitude based on what we have or what we hope to receive, but a deep, soul-rooted thanksgiving for who God is and the simple joy of being known by Him.

Contemplative prayer might begin with a simple phrase or scripture whispered in the heart—"Thank You, Lord," or "Your mercy endures forever." And then we wait. We breathe. We listen. We allow that single thought to draw us into a deeper awareness of His presence. Sometimes we feel overwhelmed with peace. Sometimes tears fall without explanation. Other times, we simply sit in silence, trusting that even when we feel nothing, God is working in the quiet places of our hearts.

It is in this silence that gratitude takes root. It becomes more than a feeling—it becomes part of our spiritual DNA, shaping how we see the world, how we respond to hardship, and how we relate to others. When we rest in the loving gaze of the Father, our hearts cannot help but respond with awe and thanksgiving.

Contemplative prayer is also healing. It reminds us that we don't have to perform for God. We don't have to impress Him with eloquent words or lengthy prayers. He simply wants our presence— our willingness to draw near, to sit with Him, and to listen. In that space, we find rest. And in that rest, we find gratitude.

It's often in contemplative prayer that our greatest transformation takes place. Not because we are actively working on ourselves, but because we are placing ourselves before the One who does the transforming. As the psalmist said, *"Those who look to Him are radiant"* (Psalm 34:5). As we gaze upon the beauty of the Lord, His peace fills us, His love reshapes us, and His goodness stirs a gratitude we couldn't have mustered on our own.

If you've never practiced this kind of prayer before, start simply. Find a quiet place. Take a few deep breaths. Whisper a name of God that reminds you of His goodness— *"Shepherd," "Father," "Redeemer," "Friend."* Let that name linger in your thoughts. And then, simply be with Him. Sit in the sacred silence and let gratitude rise like a gentle tide in your soul.

Contemplative prayer is not about results; it is about relationship. It's about intimacy with God, a love that is not rushed or rehearsed, but real and restful. And it is in that place—unhurried, unhindered, and holy—that gratitude is no longer something we do, but something we become.

Intercessory Prayer Infused with Gratitude

Intercessory prayer—lifting the needs of others before the throne of God—is one of the most beautiful and selfless forms of prayer. It is the act of standing in the gap, of bearing one another's burdens in love, and of partnering with God to bring about His will in the lives of those we care about. But when intercession is joined with gratitude, it becomes even more powerful. It becomes not just a plea, but a proclamation of faith.

Rather than simply asking for God's intervention, we begin by thanking Him for who He is—faithful, good, merciful, and sovereign. We thank Him for how He is already moving, even when we cannot yet see the outcome. We thank Him for the people we are praying for—their lives, their stories, the very breath in their lungs. Gratitude grounds our intercession in hope, and it reminds us that God is not distant or indifferent, but already present and at work.

This practice transforms the tone of our prayers. Instead of praying from a place of desperation, we pray from a place of confidence—believing in God's character, trusting His timing, and remembering

His past faithfulness. It turns our gaze from fear to faith. Rather than simply pleading, we begin praising.

Consider the difference between these two prayers:

"Lord, please heal my friend. I'm afraid for them. I don't know what to do."

"Lord, thank You for being the Great Physician. Thank You for the ways You've already sustained my friend. I trust You are working even now, and I ask that You bring Your healing and peace."

The second prayer acknowledges the very real need while also declaring faith in the One who meets it. Gratitude keeps us from praying as if we are trying to twist God's arm. Instead, we approach Him as beloved children, confident in His love and His willingness to respond.

I've often found that my prayers for others become more intimate and more effective when I begin by thanking God for those individuals by name. I thank Him for their presence in my life, for the ways they've impacted me, for the image of Christ I see in them. This posture of gratitude not only blesses them—it transforms me. It softens my heart, deepens my compassion, and ignites my faith.

There is also something sacred about thanking God in advance. When we pray, "Lord, I thank You for how You will work in this situation," we are aligning our hearts with His promises. We are saying, "God, I believe You are faithful even before I see the answer." That kind of faith-filled gratitude stirs the heavens.

The Apostle Paul modeled this beautifully. In nearly every one of his letters, he began by thanking God for the people he was writing to—even when they were facing trials, even when they were struggling. He wrote in Philippians 1:3–4,

"I thank my God every time I remember you. In all my prayers for all of you, I always pray with joy."

What a powerful way to intercede: with thanksgiving, with joy, with confidence in God's love.

In your own prayer life, try pairing every intercession with an expression of thanks. Thank God for the opportunity to pray. Thank Him for His promises. Thank Him for the life of the one you're lifting up. And when the answer comes—whether it looks as you expected or not—thank Him again, trusting that He has worked in His perfect wisdom.

Intercessory prayer infused with gratitude is not just about changing circumstances—it's about changing hearts, starting with our own. It invites us to walk in faith, to speak life, and to stand firm in the assurance that our God is both listening and already moving.

Let us become people who pray with both urgency and thankfulness—who believe not only in God's power to act, but in His presence that sustains. And as we lift others up, may we also lift up hearts full of gratitude, trusting that He who began a good work is faithful to complete it.

Scriptural Prayers of Thanksgiving

One of my favorite ways to pray is by using Scripture, and there's no better source for prayers of thanksgiving than the Psalms. David's heart overflows with gratitude throughout these powerful passages, offering us a model for heartfelt praise.

But we don't have to look only to the Psalms to find meaningful scriptures to incorporate into our prayers. Consider these powerful verses:

The Key to a Life of Peace and Purpose

Psalm 107:8-9 – *"Let them give thanks to the Lord for His unfailing love and His wonderful deeds for mankind, for He satisfies the thirsty and fills the hungry with good things."*

Psalm 95:2 – *"Let's come before Him with thanksgiving; let's shout songs of joy to Him!"*

Psalm 116:1-2 – *"I love the Lord, because He has heard my voice and my supplications. Because He has inclined His ear to me, therefore I will call upon Him as long as I live."*

1 Chronicles 16:34 – *"Give thanks to the Lord, for He is good; His love endures forever."*

Colossians 3:17 – *"And whatever you do, whether in word or deed, do it all in the name of the Lord Jesus, giving thanks to God the Father through Him."*

Praying through these scriptures allows our gratitude to be shaped by God's Word, grounding us in His promises and unwavering faithfulness. As we declare His goodness through His own words, our hearts are drawn closer to Him, and our spirit is strengthened by the truth of His love.

(For additional help on praying and meditating on scripture, I've included a list for reference at the end of this book)

Daily Acts of Thankful Prayer

Prayer infused with gratitude is not limited to set moments—it can become a constant rhythm woven into the fabric of our day. Paul reminds us in 1 Thessalonians 5:16-18,

"Rejoice always, pray without ceasing, give thanks in all circumstances; for this is the will of God in Christ Jesus for you."

At first glance, the idea of praying *without ceasing* may seem overwhelming. How could anyone possibly pray all the time? But this instruction is not about spending every waking moment in formal prayer—it's about the condition of the heart. When our hearts are in tune with God, prayer becomes as natural as breathing. It is not about reciting words endlessly, but about cultivating an ongoing awareness of His presence, turning to Him in every moment—whether in need, gratitude, or simple recognition of His goodness.

Just yesterday, I received an email regarding a woman who has been working on a project for the ministry where I serve. The message informed me that our project would be delayed because her husband had been hospitalized and placed on life support. As I sat in my office reading those words, I found myself immediately bursting into prayer—aloud, unashamed, and unconcerned with who might hear. My heart ached for this woman, and there was no hesitation in turning to God on her behalf. It wasn't a scheduled prayer time, nor did I stop to compose my thoughts. It was simply an instinctive response—a heart aligned with the Father, moved by compassion, and reaching out in faith.

In the same way, prayers of thanksgiving can rise from our hearts throughout the day. When we walk in close relationship with the Savior, gratitude becomes second nature. We begin to see blessings everywhere—in the beauty of the morning light, in the kindness of a stranger, in the small victories that remind us God is at work. And when our hearts are full of gratitude, those praises cannot be contained. They spill out in whispered prayers, in spontaneous songs of praise, in quiet moments of awe at His faithfulness.

But let me be clear—I am not some pious do-gooder, nor am I trying to paint myself as a saint. I am simply a man who has been relentlessly pursued by God, even after failing miserably. I once allowed pride to lead me into the depths of sin, and that path took me straight into the darkness of federal prison. It was there, in the dead of night, that the Holy Spirit met me, broke through my hardened heart, and led me back to the Father. I know what it is to be lost, to be utterly broken, to sit in the wreckage of my own choices. But I also know what it is to be redeemed, to be lifted out of that pit and set on solid ground once again.

That's why I live differently now. My heart overflows with gratitude—not the kind that comes from having an easy life, but the kind that only a condemned and broken soul, restored by the mercy of God, could ever truly understand. Every prayer I whisper, every breath of thanksgiving, is a response to the grace that rescued me. And so, I pray—not because I have to, but because I *can't help it.*

The Key to a Life of Peace and Purpose

Because gratitude has transformed my heart, and prayer has become the language of my soul.

CHAPTER EIGHT:

REMOVING BARRIERS
TO A GRATEFUL HEART

Cultivating a heart of gratitude is not always easy. While we may desire to live with thankfulness, deeply ingrained emotions such as guilt, shame, and resentment can create barriers that prevent gratitude from flourishing. These emotions, often shaped by past wounds or present struggles, can cloud our ability to recognize and receive the blessings in our lives. But true gratitude does not require us to ignore these struggles—it invites us to acknowledge them, work through them, and, ultimately, find healing and freedom in God's grace.

The Key to a Life of Peace and Purpose

Gratitude, at its core, is not about pretending that life is without pain. It is about choosing to see God's goodness even in the midst of difficulty, trusting that His hand is still at work. Psalm 34:18 reminds us,

"The Lord is close to the brokenhearted and saves those who are crushed in spirit."

God does not ask us to suppress our pain but to bring it to Him, allowing Him to heal what is wounded and restore what has been lost.

My dear sister, Diane, to whom this book is dedicated, spoke of this very truth just yesterday as we talked on the phone. For years, she had struggled with depression, anger, and uncontrollable bouts of crying. The weight of long-buried pain had surfaced—pain rooted in the abuse she suffered at the hands of men esteemed by our parents. The first time it happened; she was very young. Frightened and confused, she confided in one of our siblings, who immediately informed our mother. But instead of protection, Diane was met with punishment. The man who had harmed her was respected, and rather than being believed, she was accused of lying.

Cultivating Gratitude

When, years later, our step-grandfather, held in high regard by our father, began to abuse her in the same way, she remained silent. She had learned that her cries would not be heard, that her pain would not be acknowledged. And so, she carried the agony alone, bearing a burden no child should ever have to bear.

By the time she turned thirteen, the weight of it all became too much. Depression consumed her, anger became her defense, and both took root deep within her spirit, shaping her emotions and controlling her responses. This battle raged on for decades, even into her years as a pastor's wife. She loved the Lord, yet she wrestled with the pain that refused to loosen its grip. Even as she built a life and raised her children, the wounds remained, festering beneath the surface.

It wasn't until her children reached their preteen years that she realized the full extent of what that anger was doing to her. One day, overwhelmed by frustration, she felt herself lashing out at her children in ways that frightened her. The weight of it all—the years of silence, the unhealed wounds, the simmering rage—threatened to crush her.

Desperate, she retreated to her bedroom, fell upon her face, and cried out to God for deliverance.

And graciously, God met her there.

As she lay broken before Him, she felt His voice—not an audible sound, but a deep, undeniable truth stirring within her spirit. *"If you give Me your anger, I will heal you."*

In that moment, she knew what she had to do. With everything in her, she surrendered. "Lord, I give You my anger," she cried, and as she spoke those words, she began to give thanks—thanking God not only for hearing her but for the healing she believed He was already bringing.

And in His mercy, He did.

From that moment on, Diane was set free. The anger that had defined her for so long, the bitterness that had stolen so much of her joy, was lifted. God had not erased her past, but He had healed her heart.

Today, if you sit with her, you will feel the depth of her gratitude. She speaks with tenderness of the husband who walked beside her through the years of pain and depression, never wavering in his love for her. She lifts her voice in constant praise, giving glory to the God who redeemed her suffering and replaced her pain with peace.

Her story is a testimony to the power of surrender, the power of gratitude, and the boundless grace of God. Because when we bring our deepest wounds before Him, He is faithful to heal—and when we give thanks, even in the midst of our pain, we make room for His restoring love to do its work.

Overcoming Guilt Through Grace

One of the greatest barriers to gratitude is guilt—the feeling that we are unworthy of the blessings we receive. Perhaps we are burdened by past mistakes, weighed down by failures, or struggling with regret over missed opportunities. Left unchecked, guilt can make us believe that we are undeserving of God's goodness, causing us to reject or minimize His blessings rather than receiving them with a thankful heart.

The antidote to guilt is grace. God's love is not dependent on our perfection but on His mercy. *1 John 1:9* assures us,

The Key to a Life of Peace and Purpose

"If we confess our sins, He is faithful and just and will forgive us our sins and purify us from all unrighteousness."

Gratitude begins when we accept that we are not defined by our past but by God's unchanging grace.

If guilt is a struggle, take time in prayer to seek forgiveness—not only from God but also from yourself. Write a letter of confession and release, acknowledging your mistakes but also recognizing God's willingness to redeem them. Remember that His mercies are new every morning (*Lamentations 3:22-23*), and His grace is sufficient for you (*2 Corinthians 12:9*).

Letting Go of Shame and Embracing Self-Worth

Shame is a heavy burden, far deeper and more destructive than guilt. While guilt whispers, "I have done something wrong," shame shouts, "I am wrong." It twists our self-perception, making us believe that we are fundamentally flawed, unworthy of love, and beyond redemption. When shame takes root, it blinds us to our value, silences our joy, and hinders our ability to receive and appreciate the goodness in our lives.

But God does not see us through the lens of shame. He sees us as His beloved children—redeemed, cherished, and made whole in Christ. Romans 8:1 declares, "There is now no condemnation for those who are in Christ Jesus." If we struggle with feelings of unworthiness, we must replace the lies of shame with the truth of our identity in Christ.

One powerful way to combat shame is through speaking and meditating on scripture-based affirmations:

"I am fearfully and wonderfully made." (Psalm 139:14)

"I am chosen and dearly loved." (Colossians 3:12)

"I am a new creation in Christ." (2 Corinthians 5:17)

When we immerse ourselves in these truths, our inner narrative begins to change. Gratitude no longer flows from a place of striving or self-condemnation but from a heart that knows it is loved, forgiven, and restored.

Absorbing this truth was one of the most difficult journeys of my life. Having fallen headlong into the sin of pride, I did the unthinkable. I betrayed the trust of others, wounded people I loved, and abandoned my family—all in a desperate, misguided attempt at self-preservation. The consequences were severe. I found myself stripped of everything I once held dear, serving eight years in federal prison.

Shame? I wore it like a cloak, suffocating and relentless. Forgiveness? I couldn't even imagine it. To forgive myself felt impossible. And the thought of being forgiven by a God I had spent over five years blaming for my downfall? Utterly inconceivable.

But God is not like us. He is relentless in His mercy, unyielding in His love, and unshakable in His grace. He pursued me to the lowest place, into the shadows where no one else could reach me. And there, in the stillness of a prison cell, the Holy Spirit met me. Like David, I came undone. One merciful night, I confessed my sins before Him—every one of them—and I knew in my mind that I was forgiven.

But the distance from head to heart can be long and painful.

It took four more years before I could fully receive that truth in my spirit—before I could stop identifying myself by my failure and start embracing the identity God had written for me. That I was no longer condemned. That I was free. That I was His.

When I hear songs like Katy Nicole's, *"God is in This Story"*, or Zack Willams', *"There was Jesus"*, I can't help but lift my voice in praise and thanksgiving. The chains of my past no longer define me. The voice of shame has been silenced. There is no more condemnation in my spirit—I am a new creation, a beloved child of the Most High King.

Just when I thought my life was over—when I was ready to close the book and write "The End" over my story—the Author of my soul picked up His pen and began to write a new chapter. A chapter not defined by regret, but by redemption. Not shaped by shame, but by grace. I was no longer enslaved to the memory of my mistakes. I was no longer bound by the weight of who I had been.

He gave me a new name. A new purpose. A new story to tell.

And friend, if He did that for me... He can do the same for you.

Releasing Resentment Through Forgiveness

Resentment, whether directed toward others or ourselves, can be one of the most significant barriers to gratitude. When we hold onto bitterness, we remain tethered to past hurts, unable to fully appreciate the blessings of the present. Forgiveness is not about dismissing pain or excusing wrongdoing; it is about freeing our hearts from the weight of anger and making space for gratitude to grow.

Jesus modeled this kind of forgiveness on the cross when He prayed,

"Father, forgive them, for they do not know what they are doing" (Luke 23:34).

If He could extend grace in the face of ultimate betrayal, we too are called to release the burdens of resentment, trusting that God is our healer and our vindicator.

If resentment lingers, take time to pray for those who have wronged you. Ask God for the strength to forgive, even if the feelings do not immediately follow. Over time, forgiveness softens the heart, allowing gratitude to replace bitterness with peace.

CHAPTER NINE:

OVERCOMING DEPRESSION WITH GRATITUDE

There is no denying that some dear souls suffer deeply from depression brought on by mental illness. I know this pain personally, as my own grandfather wrestled with it in such a profound way that, in a moment of despair, he took his life when my father was just twelve years old. That devastating loss left a lasting wound on my father's heart, and in many ways, it became the root of his own struggle with sorrow. While Dad's depression wasn't as severe or clinical as his father's, it was no less real. His sadness sprang from a place of grief and long-held self-pity—a heavy burden carried from childhood.

Scripture reminds us in Ephesians 6:12 that;
"

"We do not wrestle against flesh and blood, but against principalities, against powers, against the rulers of the darkness of this age."

The enemy will use whatever tools he can to distract, discourage, and detour us from walking fully in the calling God has placed on our lives. Depression is one of those tools—a thief of joy, a silencer of praise, a fog that clouds our vision of God's goodness.

But I witnessed a powerful transformation in my father when he began to shift his focus from what was lost to what remained. As he recommitted himself to the ministry God had entrusted to him, and as he began to cultivate a spirit of gratitude toward the Savior who had rescued him from the depths of sin, the depression lost its grip. The darkness gave way to light.

This is not to say the journey was easy or instant. But the principle is simple: depression feeds on self-focus, on what we think we lack, what we've missed, or what might have been. Gratitude, however, shifts our attention outward—toward God, toward others, and toward the gifts we've already received.

Paul's exhortation in Romans 12:2 echoes this:

"Be transformed by the renewing of your mind, that you may prove what is that good and acceptable and perfect will of God."

And again, in Philippians 4:8, he provides a roadmap for where our thoughts should dwell:

"Finally, brothers, whatever is true, whatever is honorable, whatever is just, whatever is pure, whatever is lovely, whatever is commendable, if there is any excellence, if there is anything worthy of praise, think about these things."

The battle for joy is often fought in the mind. Depression grows when we dwell on *"what ifs"*, on wrongs committed against us, or on the negative voices that speak discouragement and defeat. But when we choose to reframe our thinking, focusing on what is good, what is true, and what is praiseworthy, gratitude begins to blossom, and in that sacred space, depression loses its footing.

Now, don't misunderstand me. Believers are not immune to depression. Christians struggle too. But we have something the world cannot offer: a Savior who heals, a Word that restores, and a spiritual family to walk alongside us in our pain. We are not alone in this fight. We have the hope of Christ, the truth of Scripture, and the prayers and support of the Church.

Much of our ability to live in gratitude begins with how we choose to think. If our thoughts are always fixed on what we lack or fear, we will miss the blessings that surround us. But Scripture calls us to a different way, a renewed mind, one that is anchored in faith, not fear; abundance, not scarcity.

One simple and practical way to renew our thinking is by training our minds to see situations through a lens of gratitude:

The Power of Affirmation in Cultivating Gratitude

One of the most overlooked, yet incredibly effective tools in the fight against depression is the practice of positive affirmation. Speaking words of life, especially those rooted in Scripture and truth, is not merely a motivational exercise, it's a spiritual discipline that has the power to reshape how we think, feel, and respond to life.

Science confirms what Scripture has long declared: *what we meditate on, we become.* When we consistently speak words of gratitude, truth, and hope, we are engaging in a process called neuroplasticity—the brain's remarkable ability to form new neural pathways. Just as negative thoughts can dig deep ruts of despair, *positive affirmations can carve out paths of peace, purpose, and thanksgiving.*

When you declare daily truths like, *"God is my provider,"* or *"I am loved, chosen, and redeemed,"* or *"I trust that God is working all things for my good,"* you are not just hoping for a better mindset—you are *training your mind to believe it.*

Instead of waking up overwhelmed with worry about what might go wrong, start your day with a simple spoken affirmation of thanksgiving: *"Lord, I thank You that Your mercies are new this morning." "I thank You that You are with me today, and You will supply all my needs. I may not feel strong right now, but I thank You that Your strength is made perfect in my weakness."*

The Key to a Life of Peace and Purpose

These declarations are not wishful thinking; they are *faith in action*. When repeated consistently, they begin to transform not only your thoughts but your emotional response to daily challenges. Gratitude becomes the default rather than the exception. Peace begins to guard your heart. Purpose starts to rise again.

As mentioned earlier, the Apostle Paul understood this principle well when he wrote in Philippians 4:8 to *"think on these things..."*—things that are true, noble, right, pure, lovely, admirable, excellent, and praiseworthy. In other words, he was encouraging us to speak and think in alignment with the goodness of God. Affirmation, when guided by Scripture, is one of the most powerful tools we have for renewing our minds.

If you're battling depression or anxiety, begin this practice—not out of obligation, but as an act of defiant hope. Choose one or two truths rooted in Scripture. Speak them out loud in the morning, at lunch, in the mirror, or before bed. Let your own voice be the reminder of what God has spoken over your life.

Let affirmation become the echo of heaven in your day. Let it be the gentle, persistent nudge that steers your heart back toward gratitude. And in doing so, you will find your thoughts renewed, your burdens lightened, and your spirit lifted—one faithful word at a time.

The God of Promise, The God of Peace

When we intentionally seek out the good, we will begin to see God's fingerprints even in the most unlikely places. And as we do, our hearts will shift from heaviness to hope—from despair to gratitude.

Let us hold fast to the truth that even in the valley, God is near, and through His presence and His promises, we can find joy again. The writer of Hebrews tells us;

"Let us hold fast the confession of our hope without wavering, for He who promised is faithful."
Hebrews 10:23

So, what are the promises that we can hold onto to help us overcome the onslaught of the enemy? Let us go back to Philippians 4:8, as quoted

The Key to a Life of Peace and Purpose

previously in this chapter, and read it in context with verses 6 and 7:

"do not be anxious about anything, but in everything by prayer and supplication with thanksgiving let your requests be made known to God. And the peace of God, which surpasses all understanding, will guard your hearts and your minds in Christ Jesus."

This peace that Paul describes is not merely the absence of turmoil—it is the active presence of God's comfort and assurance. It's the kind of peace that shows up not because the storm has passed, but because we've chosen to anchor ourselves in the One who calms the wind and waves. It is peace that *guards*—like a sentinel at the gates of our heart and mind—shielding us from the despair that seeks to creep in.

Gratitude, then, becomes more than a pleasant habit. It becomes a lifeline. When we give thanks in the midst of our pain, we're not denying the struggle, we're declaring that the struggle does not have the final word. We are proclaiming, with thanksgiving, that God is still in control, still good, and still working on our behalf.

Cultivating Gratitude

One of the most beautiful aspects of this passage in Philippians is that Paul doesn't lay this out as a lofty ideal, but as a practical path. Don't worry. Pray. Be thankful. Make your requests known. And then—*then*—the peace of God, which defies logic and transcends understanding, will step in and protect your inner life.

This is what we're invited to do in our darkest moments—not to muster strength on our own, but to surrender our burdens with thanksgiving. And in return, our faithful Father surrounds us with His peace.

We must also remember that gratitude is not something we wait to feel, it is something we choose to practice. Especially when emotions fail us. Especially when the world feels heavy. We give thanks not because everything is good, but because *God* is good. And when we train our hearts to see His hand at work, even in the broken places, we begin to live from a place of quiet trust.

So, when the weight of depression presses in— when grief lingers, or fear grips, or memories haunt—return to this promise:

The Key to a Life of Peace and Purpose

"The peace of God... will guard your hearts and minds in Christ Jesus."

Let that be your confession. Let that be your hope. And let gratitude be the door you continue to walk through, again and again, until the light begins to break through.

This is exactly what happened when my sister Diane went before God with her anger, as I shared in Chapter Four. Years of suffering in silence had left her carrying a heavy burden—one rooted in pain, injustice, and a sense of betrayal. That weight manifested in anger and deep emotional turmoil, coloring her responses and robbing her of peace.

But there came a day, in the quiet of her bedroom, where she laid it all before the Lord. Broken, weary, and desperate for healing, she fell to her knees and cried out to God—not with eloquent words or polished prayers, but with raw honesty and surrender. And in that sacred moment, God met her. Not with condemnation, but with mercy. Not with demands, but with an invitation.

The peace came—and it stayed. That unexplainable, all-surpassing peace Paul wrote of became her reality.

Cultivating Gratitude

To this day, Diane continues to walk in that healing. The peace continues to guard her heart and her mind, and as a result, genuine, hard won, gratitude flows from her heart. She continually gives thanks—not only for what God has delivered her from, but for the way He walked with her through it.

This, dear reader, is the power of surrender mingled with gratitude. When we release the pain we've been gripping so tightly, and lift up a prayer of thanksgiving—even if it's through tears—God exchanges our anguish for peace. He trades our despair for hope. And slowly, quietly, our hearts begin to heal.

So when Paul says, "with thanksgiving, let your requests be made known to God," he is not prescribing a surface-level positivity. He's pointing us toward a deep, soul-level trust that even in our hardest moments, God is near—and He is enough. Gratitude, then, becomes the doorway through which healing enters. Peace becomes the gift we never expected but where peace dwells, depression no longer has a foothold. God's faithfulness becomes the testimony we carry into every chapter of our life that follows.

The Key to a Life of Peace and Purpose

n the battle against depression, especially the kind rooted in persistent negative thoughts, gratitude becomes a powerful weapon—not because it denies pain, but because it shifts our focus to what is true, good, and worthy of praise. As we discussed earlier, depression often takes hold when we dwell on what is lacking or broken. But through gratitude, we reframe our thoughts, lifting our eyes from the weight of our circumstances to the faithfulness of God.

A Powerful Resource

One of the most helpful resources I've come across for those struggling with ongoing depression, is a book written by my dear friend, Marybeth Wuenschel, titled *Your Thoughts Are Killing You: Take Control of Your Mind and Close the Door to Depression, Anxiety and Those Fearful, Worrisome Thoughts Forever*, (available on Amazon). This book is a lifeline for anyone battling shame, guilt, anxiety, or the overwhelming belief that they are beyond hope.

Marybeth writes with transparency and truth, reminding us that not every thought that comes into our mind is from us—or for us. She exposes

Cultivating Gratitude

the lies we so easily believe and equips readers with tools grounded in Scripture to take every thought captive, as Paul instructs us in 2 Corinthians 10:5. Her message is clear: *You have the authority in Christ to cast down lies and live free.*

As she says, "It's just a thought"—but how often we forget that. How often we let those thoughts define us, imprison us, or convince us that we are too far gone. If that's where you find yourself today, I urge you to read her book. It's not a quick fix, but a Spirit-led invitation to partner with God in renewing your mind and finding freedom.

Jesus said in John 8:32,

"You will know the truth, and the truth will set you free."

Not simply hearing it—but knowing it, internalizing it. That's where the chains fall off.

Pairing gratitude with the truth of God's Word—as Marybeth so powerfully encourages—can lead to healing and lasting peace. Don't fight this battle alone. Let gratitude, truth, and the transforming power of Christ bring light into the dark

The Key to a Life of Peace and Purpose

places of your heart. There is hope, and there is help. And most importantly, you are not alone.

CHAPTER TEN:

SUSTAINING A LIFE OF GRATITUDE

Ultimately, gratitude is not about waiting for life to be perfect—it is about choosing to see God's goodness in every moment. It is about shifting our focus from what is missing to what is present, from what is broken to what is being restored.

Jesus gave thanks before performing miracles (*John 6:11*). Paul gave thanks while imprisoned (*Philippians 1:3-6*). Job worshiped in the midst of loss (*Job 1:21*). Their gratitude was not based on circumstances but on the unshakable truth that God is faithful.

The Key to a Life of Peace and Purpose

Let us remember that gratitude is a journey, one that requires patience, persistence, and faith. It is not about denying pain but about trusting that joy is still possible. It is not about ignoring struggles but about recognizing that even in the darkness, there is light.

So let us choose gratitude. Not just in moments of abundance, but in every season. Not just when life is easy, but when it is hard. Not just in times of certainty, but in times of waiting.

For when we choose gratitude, we step into the fullness of God's presence, experiencing the peace, joy, and purpose He has promised.

Once again we're reminded in *1 Thessalonians 5:18* :

"Give thanks in all circumstances; for this is God's will for you in Christ Jesus."

Building a sustainable gratitude practice is not a sprint—it is a marathon, a lifelong journey of intentional awareness and appreciation. While initial enthusiasm can propel us forward, the reality is that daily routines, responsibilities, and unforeseen challenges can cause gratitude to fade into the background. This is perfectly natural. The key is to develop strategies that anchor gratitude in your daily life, allowing it to become not just a passing emotion but a way of seeing, thinking, and living.

Gratitude, much like faith, must be cultivated with diligence. Jesus spoke of this kind of perseverance in *Matthew 7:24-25*, comparing a wise person to one who builds their house on a solid foundation. When the storms of life come, that house remains standing. Likewise, when gratitude is deeply ingrained in our hearts and minds, it becomes a steady foundation that sustains us, even in life's difficult seasons.

Making Gratitude a Daily Habit

One of the most effective ways to nurture a lasting gratitude practice is by weaving it into the fabric of your daily life. Gratitude should never feel like an obligation; rather, it should become a natural rhythm—a quiet moment of reflection, a whispered prayer, a simple act of appreciation.

Consider beginning your mornings with a few minutes of thanksgiving. Before reaching for your phone or rushing into the day's responsibilities, take a deep breath and simply thank God for the gift of a new day.

I am reminded of Pastor Shoemake, a man who pastored in San Jose, California. I only came to know him in his later years, but what struck me most was his sensitivity to the Holy Spirit and his deep humility. He radiated compassion, carrying a love for people that I had rarely witnessed before.

One morning, as I sat with him, he shared something that has stayed with me ever since. He said, *"Jesse, the first words I speak every morning when I wake up are, 'I love You, Jesus.'"*

Why those words? Because his heart was so full of gratitude that he couldn't start his day without expressing it to the One to whom he owed everything. He lived a life of thanksgiving. When he prayed, you could feel the depth of that gratitude— he gave thanks for everything: for shelter, for warmth, for peace, and most of all, for the redemption purchased by the blood of Christ.

If we begin our days as Pastor Shoemake did, we will find it easier to continue in gratitude throughout the day. We will pause more often to recognize small blessings—the kindness of a stranger, a moment of laughter, the beauty of a sunset.

Cultivating Gratitude

And as we prepare to lay our heads down at night, gratitude can be the final thought on our lips—a quiet reflection on the day's gifts, a simple acknowledgment of God's presence in each moment. The more we cultivate this habit, the more natural it becomes, until thanksgiving is not just something we practice—it is the very posture of our hearts.

The Apostle Paul encouraged the believers in *Colossians 3:17,*

"And whatever you do, whether in word or deed, do it all in the name of the Lord Jesus, giving thanks to God the Father through Him."

This verse reminds us that gratitude is not limited to special moments—it is something we can integrate into everything we do.

Consistency: The Key to Lasting Practice

Gratitude flourishes when it becomes a habit. Like any spiritual discipline, it requires repetition and commitment. Setting aside even five minutes a day can create a lasting impact. Some find that a

The Key to a Life of Peace and Purpose

morning gratitude journal sets a positive tone for the day, while others prefer reflecting on blessings before bed. Experiment with different approaches and find what best aligns with your daily life.

Yet, as with any habit, there will be days when gratitude feels distant. It is in these moments that perseverance matters most. If you struggle to find something to be grateful for, start small, thank God for your health, your meal, the air you breathe...

Jesus reminded His followers in *Luke 16:10*,

"Whoever can be trusted with very little can also be trusted with much."

When we train ourselves to be grateful for small things, our hearts become more attuned to God's greater blessings.

Surrounding Yourself with Gratitude Reminders

Visual reminders can reinforce gratitude in daily life. Place a gratitude journal by your bedside. Display scripture verses about thankfulness on your walls, mirrors, or workspaces. Create a gratitude jar where you jot down moments of thanksgiving on slips of paper and review them at the end of each month.

A powerful way to reinforce gratitude is by sharing it with others. Talk about your blessings with friends, family, or your faith community. Encourage one another by speaking words of appreciation and testifying to the goodness of God. As *Hebrews 10:24-25* urges us,

"Let us consider how we may spur one another on toward love and good deeds, not giving up meeting together... but encouraging one another."

A Lifelong Commitment to Gratitude

Sustaining gratitude is not about achieving perfection—it is about walking in awareness, embracing both the joys and challenges of life with a heart that trusts in God's goodness.

There will be seasons when gratitude flows easily and seasons when it is a discipline requiring effort. But each time we choose thanksgiving, we draw closer to the abundant life God desires for us.

The Key to a Life of Peace and Purpose

"Let the peace of Christ rule in your hearts, since as members of one body you were called to peace. And be thankful." (Colossians 3:15)

May we commit to living each day with gratitude, knowing that in doing so, we open our hearts to deeper joy, greater faith, and an ever-growing awareness of God's love.

CHAPTER ELEVEN:

THE POWER OF GRATITUDE IN ACTION

Acts of service are one of the most profound and tangible ways to express gratitude. While words carry weight, actions often speak even louder, demonstrating appreciation in a way that resonates deeply. True gratitude is not only about what we say—it is about how we live, how we show our appreciation through selfless acts of kindness, and how we use our time and talents to bless others.

Jesus Himself exemplified this principle in His ministry. In *Mark 10:45*, He declares,

The Key to a Life of Peace and Purpose

"For even the Son of Man did not come to be served, but to serve, and to give His life as a ransom for many."

His life was the ultimate model of love in action, demonstrating that service is a powerful expression of gratitude—not only to God but also to those around us.

The Heart Behind the Act

The beauty of acts of service lies not in their size or visibility but in the sincerity and intention behind them. A grand gesture done with selfish motives holds little value, but a small act done with love can transform lives. *1 Corinthians 13:3* reminds us,

"If I give all I possess to the poor and give over my body to hardship that I may boast, but do not have love, I gain nothing."

True service is not about seeking recognition but about genuine care for others.

For instance, consider a mother exhausted from the responsibilities of raising children. While verbal encouragement is helpful, taking action—whether by babysitting, preparing a meal, or offering a quiet moment of respite—demonstrates a deeper level of appreciation. Similarly, a colleague overwhelmed by a heavy workload may feel encouraged by kind words, but offering practical support, like helping with a task or brainstorming solutions, expresses gratitude in a more impactful way.

Simple Acts, Lasting Impact

Acts of service do not have to be elaborate. Sometimes, the smallest gestures have the most significant effects. The key is to notice the needs of those around us and respond with kindness. Whether the service involves helping around the house offering to help a friend move, supporting a colleague at work, or serving in the community it can be a blessing and encouragement to someone else, promoting gratitude in their hearts.

Jesus set the perfect example in *John 13:12-17* when He washed His disciples' feet—an act of service that demonstrated humility and love. He then instructed them to do the same for others, teaching that serving with gratitude is not just a one-time action but a way of life.

Serving Without Expectation

True acts of service are given freely, without expectation of recognition or return. Luke 6:35 reminds us,

"But love your enemies, do good to them, and lend to them without expecting to get anything back. Then your reward will be great, and you will be children of the Most High."

Service should never be driven by obligation or self-interest, but rather by a heart overflowing with generosity and gratitude.

Think about how radical Jesus' words truly are. Not only does He call us to love our enemies, but He tells us to do good to them. Then—just when we think we understand—He takes it a step further, challenging even our finances. *Lend to them, expecting nothing in return?* Wait... what?!

It is easy to serve when we know our efforts will be appreciated. A heartfelt "thank you" can be affirming, and recognition can be rewarding. But the true test of a servant's heart is the willingness to serve even when no one notices. That is where real transformation takes place—when we give, not for applause, but out of the simple, pure gratitude for the opportunity to bless others.

Serving as an Expression of Faith

For believers, acts of service are not just good deeds; they are expressions of faith and obedience to God. *James 2:17* reminds us,

"Faith by itself, if it is not accompanied by action, is dead."

When we serve others, we reflect God's love and gratitude for His blessings in our own lives.

Consider aligning your acts of service with your spiritual values:

Giving to the Poor: Proverbs 19:17 says,

"Whoever is kind to the poor lends to the Lord, and He will reward them for what they have done."

Encouraging the Weary: *Galatians 6:2* urges us to

"Carry each other's burdens, and in this way you will fulfill the law of Christ."

The Key to a Life of Peace and Purpose

Using Your Gifts: *1 Peter 4:10* teaches,

"Each of you should use whatever gift you have received to serve others, as faithful stewards of God's grace."

When we recognize our talents and resources as gifts from God, serving becomes a natural outpouring of gratitude.

Acts of Service in Challenging Times

There will be seasons when serving feels difficult—when life is overwhelming, energy is low, or personal challenges take priority. Yet, it is often in these moments that acts of service have the most profound impact.

Consider those who continue to serve despite hardship—the single parent who still volunteers at church, the elderly person who prays for others daily, or the individual who, despite personal struggles, takes time to encourage a friend. These small yet mighty acts of service create ripples of kindness that extend beyond what we can see.

In difficult times, acts of service do not have to be grand. Sometimes, serving means simply showing up, offering a kind word, or giving what little we can. The widow in *Mark 12:41-44* gave only two small coins, yet Jesus honored her gift because it was given with a sincere heart.

The Joy of Serving

Acts of service are not only a blessing to others but also bring profound joy and fulfillment to the giver. Jesus Himself said in *Acts 20:35*,

"It is more blessed to give than to receive."

Science even confirms this truth, helping others releases endorphins, reduces stress, and increases overall happiness.

But beyond the personal benefits, serving deepens our relationship with God. When we align our actions with His will, we experience His presence in powerful ways.

Conclusion: Serving as a Lifestyle of Gratitude

Living a life of gratitude is more than just saying "thank you"—it is about putting that thankfulness into action. Whether through small, everyday gestures or larger commitments of time and effort, acts of service reflect a heart that recognizes and appreciates the goodness of God and others.

The Key to a Life of Peace and Purpose

As *Matthew 25:40* reminds us,

"Whatever you did for one of the least of these brothers and sisters of mine, you did for me."

When we serve, we are not just expressing gratitude to people—we are offering thanks to God Himself.

Let us cultivate a lifestyle of service, one that sees needs and meets them with love. Let us serve not out of obligation, but out of a heart overflowing with gratitude. And in doing so, may we experience the profound joy of living a life that truly reflects the love of Christ.

CHAPTER TWELVE:

THE RECIPROCAL
NATURE OF GRATITUDE

Gratitude, as we have explored, is not a one-way street. It is a vibrant, reciprocal exchange that strengthens bonds, deepens relationships, and fosters a sense of interconnectedness. While expressing appreciation to others is a powerful and transformative practice, equally important is our ability to receive gratitude. This dynamic flow of giving and receiving creates a culture of mutual respect, love, and affirmation—one that enriches both the giver and the recipient.

Failing to accept gratitude gracefully can unintentionally diminish the sincerity of the giver, leaving them feeling dismissed or undervalued. Just as it is a blessing to offer thanks, it is also a blessing to receive it with humility and joy.

Jesus Himself modeled this reciprocity in His ministry. He graciously received acts of love and appreciation, whether in the form of hospitality, anointing with oil (*Luke 7:37-38*), or words of gratitude from those He healed (*Luke 17:15-19*). In doing so, He showed us that receiving gratitude is not about self-glorification—it is about affirming love, connection, and the goodness of God at work in our relationships.

Gratitude Within Families: A Cycle of Love

Nowhere is the reciprocal nature of gratitude more evident than within the family unit. Parents tirelessly provide for their children, often making countless sacrifices out of love. Yet, when a child expresses sincere gratitude—whether through words, a thoughtful gesture, or simply a hug—it nourishes the parent's heart in a way that no material reward can.

However, we as parents should never dismiss the gratitude of a child with a casual, *"It's nothing,"* or *"That's just my job,"*. Doing so can inadvertently make the child feel that their appreciation is insignificant. Over time, this may lead to an emotional disconnect, where the child no longer feels the need to express gratitude because it is not being acknowledged. A more meaningful response should sound something like this; *"That means a lot to me. I'm so glad you see how much I love you,"*. This encourages continued expressions of thankfulness and strengthens the bond between parent and child.

Similarly, children thrive when their efforts are acknowledged with gratitude. Whether it's a teenager helping with chores without being asked, a young child sharing a toy, or an adult child making time to call home, each of these acts of love deserves appreciation. A simple "I really appreciate how responsible and kind you are" reinforces their positive behavior and cultivates a family culture of mutual gratitude.

One of the greatest blessings I've had the privilege of witnessing at the ministry where I serve is the willingness of the children of missionary volunteers to continually pitch in—not only to help their own families but to support other missionary families on campus as well. Their servant-hearted attitudes reflect the gratitude and generosity modeled by their parents.

Recently, I moved from one residence to another here on site. If you've ever had to move, you probably understand how I feel—I'd almost rather have my fingernails removed with pliers than go through the hassle of packing and hauling everything from one place to another.

Thankfully, my neighbor and close friend, Ryan, volunteered to help me. When he arrived, he wasn't alone—his eight-year-old and six-year-old sons were right by his side, eager to lend a hand. Though they weren't able to carry much, their enthusiasm was undeniable. They proudly moved the smaller items they could manage and, without being asked, even volunteered to collect and stack firewood to help me get through the remainder of the Alaskan winter.

Their willingness to serve, despite their young age, was a beautiful reminder that gratitude is best taught by example. When children see acts of kindness and appreciation modeled in daily life, they naturally respond with the same generosity of spirit.

Gratitude in Friendships: Strengthening Bonds

In friendships, gratitude is the glue that binds people together. When a friend, such as Ryan, goes out of their way to help, whether by offering a listening ear during a difficult time or lending a hand with a project, accepting their kindness with warmth and appreciation strengthens the relationship.

However, dismissing or downplaying their generosity—perhaps saying, *"You didn't have to do that,"* or *"It was no big deal,"* can diminish the value of their act. A simple, *"Thank you. That meant so much to me,"* affirms their effort and deepens your connection.

Friendships thrive on reciprocity, not in the sense of keeping score, but in the natural ebb and flow of giving and receiving. One day, you may be the one in need; another day, you may be the one offering support. The key is to receive help as graciously as you give it.

Gratitude in the Workplace: Fostering a Culture of Appreciation

In professional environments, gratitude plays a crucial role in fostering teamwork, morale, and productivity. When employees feel their hard work is noticed and appreciated, they are more engaged and motivated. A simple, *"I see the effort you put into this project, and I really appreciate it,"* from a boss or colleague can make a significant difference.

However, gratitude must also be received well. If a leader continually dismisses thanks by saying, *"I'm just doing my job,"* or *"That's what I'm paid for,"* it can create a culture where appreciation feels unnecessary or unimportant. A more thoughtful response like, *"That means a lot. I really enjoy working with this team,"* fosters an environment where gratitude flows naturally in both directions.

Gratitude and Our Relationship with God

The reciprocal nature of gratitude extends beyond our human relationships—it is also central to our relationship with God. When we express thanks for the blessings in our lives, we engage in

Cultivating Gratitude

a profound act of worship. Every prayer of thanksgiving, every moment of praise, is an acknowledgment of God's goodness and provision.

But just as we express gratitude to God, He also calls us to receive His grace, love, and blessings with open hearts. Many struggle with accepting God's gifts, feeling unworthy of His love and forgiveness. Yet, Ephesians 2:8 reminds us,

"For it is by grace you have been saved, through faith—and this is not from yourselves, it is the gift of God."

Our worthiness is not dependent on our past or our failures; it is rooted in God's unchanging love.

True humility does not mean rejecting God's blessings—it means receiving them with a grateful heart and allowing them to transform our lives. When we fully accept His grace, we are empowered to extend it to others, completing the beautiful cycle of giving and receiving.

I learned this firsthand on my journey to Alaska, where I had committed to volunteering and serving in ministry. Before heading north, I made a stop in Colorado to visit lifelong friends, Craig and Donna.

The Key to a Life of Peace and Purpose

I wasn't sure when I'd see them again, so I wanted to spend a couple of days catching up before heading to the remote state that would soon become my new home.

On the third morning, as I was preparing to leave, I climbed into my truck, exchanging final goodbyes. Just as I was about to pull away, Craig suddenly said, *"Wait a minute."* He turned and headed back inside.

A couple of minutes later, he returned, walked up to me, and stuffed some bills into my pocket. *"Use this to help fund your ministry,"* he said.

Immediately, my instinct was to return the money. I knew that Craig and Donna lived on their Social Security income alone, and I couldn't imagine taking anything from them. As I reached into my pocket, ready to hand it back, I caught a glimpse of the look on Craig's face.

It was a look of hurt—not because I was rejecting the money, but because I was rejecting his gift, his sacrifice, his offering to the Lord. In that moment, I realized the only thing I could do was climb out of the truck, wrap him in a big hug, and simply say, "Thank you."

Cultivating Gratitude

His expression immediately changed. He beamed with joy, and I could see how deeply it meant to him to give. As I drove away, tears welled in my eyes—I had almost robbed him of a blessing.

Further down the road, I reached into my pocket and unfolded the bills he had placed there. Seven hundred dollars.

I wept.

I wept because I knew the sacrifice he had just made. I wept because I had been so close to refusing the blessing God had placed before me. And I wept because I saw the beauty of gratitude in its purest form; the willingness to give sacrificially, and the willingness to receive with a humble, thankful heart.

Gratitude is not just about giving—it is also about receiving. Whether it is God's grace, the kindness of a friend, or an unexpected blessing, learning to accept gifts with gratitude allows the cycle of God's love to continue, multiplying joy in both the giver and the receiver.

The Challenge of Accepting Gratitude

For some, accepting gratitude can be difficult. Many people struggle with feelings of unworthiness, believing they do not deserve praise or recognition. Others fear that receiving help will make them indebted to others. This reluctance often stems from past wounds, cultural conditioning, or a misunderstanding of humility.

However, genuine humility does not mean rejecting gratitude, it means receiving it with grace. Jesus, the ultimate model of humility, never deflected gratitude; He received it and redirected it toward God. When Mary anointed His feet with expensive perfume (*John 12:3-8*), He did not refuse her act of love. Instead, He accepted it as a beautiful expression of worship.

Likewise, when someone thanks us, our response should not be to downplay or reject their gratitude. A simple *"Thank you, I appreciate that,"* or *"That means a lot to me,"* allows both the giver and the recipient to experience the fullness of gratitude's blessing.

Receiving Help: A Strength, Not a Weakness

Another aspect of receiving gratitude is the willingness to accept help. Many people pride themselves on self-sufficiency and hesitate to lean on others, believing they must handle everything alone. But just as we are called to serve, we are also called to be open to receiving.

Paul reminds us in *Galatians 6:2*,

"Carry each other's burdens, and in this way, you will fulfill the law of Christ."

Allowing others to help us is not a sign of weakness, it is an acknowledgment of our shared humanity. When we reject help, we not only deny ourselves support but also rob others of the opportunity to express their gratitude through acts of service.

Embracing the Full Circle of Gratitude

Gratitude is not meant to be hoarded, it is meant to flow freely between people, deepening

The Key to a Life of Peace and Purpose

relationships and creating a world filled with love and appreciation. By both expressing and receiving gratitude, we participate in something greater than ourselves—a divine rhythm of giving and receiving that reflects the very heart of God.

As *1 Thessalonians 5:18* reminds us,

"Give thanks in all circumstances; for this is God's will for you in Christ Jesus."

May we learn to embrace gratitude fully—both in the giving and in the receiving—and in doing so, may we draw closer to each other and to the One who is the source of all blessings.

CHAPTER THIRTEEN:

THE BRIDGE BETWEEN GRATITUDE AND FORGIVENESS

Forgiveness, a cornerstone of spiritual growth and emotional well-being, often feels like a monumental task, especially when faced with deep-seated hurt and betrayal. It is a journey that requires patience, grace, and a conscious shift in perspective. While forgiveness and gratitude may seem like separate disciplines, they are intricately intertwined, each acting as a catalyst for the other. Gratitude, in its ability to redirect our focus from what is lacking to what is present,

The Key to a Life of Peace and Purpose

becomes a powerful tool in dismantling the walls of resentment and paving the way for true healing.

Jesus, in His ultimate act of love, demonstrated the perfect union of gratitude and forgiveness on the cross. As He endured immense suffering, He still chose to say,

"Father, forgive them, for they do not know what they are doing" (Luke 23:34).

In this moment, Jesus showed us that forgiveness is not dependent on the worthiness of the offender, but on the willingness of the heart to let go of resentment. His gratitude for the Father's love and His mission fueled His ability to forgive even in the darkest hour.

Acknowledging the Hurt: The First Step Toward Healing

Forgiveness does not begin with simply deciding to "let go" of the past. It begins with acknowledging the hurt. Pain, when buried, festers like a wound left untreated. Suppressing emotions does not lead to healing—it deepens resentment and prevents forward movement.

Cultivating Gratitude

The Psalms are filled with raw, honest expressions of pain. *Psalm 6:6-7* says,

"I am worn out from my groaning. All night long I flood my bed with weeping and drench my couch with tears. My eyes grow weak with sorrow."

The Bible does not call us to ignore our pain but to bring it into the light where God can begin His work of restoration.

When we confront our pain, we create the opportunity to release it. This does not mean we minimize our suffering or excuse the wrongdoing of others. Rather, we choose to acknowledge the impact of the hurt while also recognizing that we are not meant to be defined by it.

Shifting Perspective: Finding Gratitude in the Midst of Pain

The path to forgiveness is difficult, but gratitude serves as a powerful companion on the journey. Shifting focus from what was lost to what remains allows us to break free from the chains of bitterness. This does not mean ignoring the wrongs done to us, but rather, choosing to acknowledge the goodness that still exists in our lives.

The Key to a Life of Peace and Purpose

Paul exemplified this mindset in *Philippians 1:12-14*, where he expressed gratitude even while imprisoned, knowing that his suffering was advancing the gospel. His ability to find meaning and appreciation amid hardship allowed him to persevere with hope rather than despair.

Gratitude, when practiced consistently, helps to soften the hardened places of our hearts. It gives us the strength to release bitterness, as we begin to see that our lives are not defined by pain, but by the love and grace that still surround us.

The Transformative Power of Empathy

Gratitude not only shifts our perspective, it also fosters empathy, which is crucial for genuine forgiveness. As we become more aware of the blessings in our own lives, we also become more attuned to the struggles of others.

The person who hurt us is not just their worst moment. They, too, are broken, shaped by their own wounds, mistakes, and regrets. Recognizing this does not excuse their actions, but it helps us see them with a more compassionate heart.

Jesus understood the frailty of human nature, and His compassion for people extended even to those who sought to harm Him. In *Matthew 9:36*, we read,

"When He saw the crowds, He had compassion on them, because they were harassed and helpless, like sheep without a shepherd."

When we approach forgiveness with gratitude, we begin to see that the person who wronged us is also in need of grace. This does not mean we continue to allow toxic or harmful behavior, but it does mean we release ourselves from the burden of hatred and resentment.

Forgiveness Is a Gift We Give Ourselves

Forgiveness is often misunderstood as something we offer solely for the benefit of the other person. In reality, forgiveness is a gift we give ourselves—a choice to no longer be weighed down by bitterness.

The Key to a Life of Peace and Purpose

Holding onto resentment does not punish the offender; it only prolongs our own suffering. *Proverbs 17:22* tells us,

"A cheerful heart is good medicine, but a crushed spirit dries up the bones."

Unforgiveness can drain us emotionally, spiritually, and even physically.

Choosing to forgive—especially when fueled by gratitude—breaks these chains. It frees us to move forward, unhindered by the past, and opens the door for peace to take root in our hearts.

Self-Forgiveness: Embracing Grace for Ourselves

Sometimes, the hardest person to forgive is ourselves. We replay past mistakes, dwell on regrets, and hold ourselves to impossible standards. Yet, if God, in His infinite love, has forgiven us, who are we to withhold forgiveness from ourselves?

1 John 1:9 assures us,

Cultivating Gratitude

"If we confess our sins, He is faithful and just and will forgive us our sins and purify us from all unrighteousness."

God's forgiveness is immediate and complete. He does not remind us of our past failures—He removes them as far as the east is from the west (*Psalm 103:12*).

Just as we extend kindness and grace to others, we must learn to extend it to ourselves.

Walking in Freedom

Forgiveness, fueled by gratitude, is a journey of freedom. It does not erase the past, but it releases its hold over us. It allows us to move forward, unburdened by bitterness, and to embrace the abundant life that God desires for us.

Colossians 3:13-14 reminds us,

"Bear with each other and forgive one another if any of you has a grievance against someone. Forgive as the Lord forgave you. And over all these virtues put on love, which binds them all together in perfect unity."

The Key to a Life of Peace and Purpose

May we choose gratitude as our foundation, forgiveness as our path, and love as our destination. For in doing so, we reflect the heart of Christ, and we walk boldly into a future filled with healing, peace, and joy.

CHAPTER FOURTEEN:

THE TRANSFORMATIVE POWER OF GRATITUDE IN RELATIONSHIPS

The transformative power of gratitude extends far beyond personal well-being; it acts as a potent catalyst for strengthening relationships of all kinds. While forgiveness lays the groundwork for reconciliation, gratitude serves as the fertile soil in which deeper connections flourish. It is not simply about saying "thank you," but about cultivating a heartfelt appreciation for the presence and contributions of others in our lives. This conscious practice of acknowledging and celebrating the good in our relationships fosters a sense of mutual respect, understanding, and love that transcends even the most challenging circumstances.

Gratitude is especially vital in romantic partnerships. Couples who consciously integrate gratitude into their daily interactions. A simple "thank you" for doing the dishes, an expression of appreciation for a thoughtful gesture, or a heartfelt compliment can go a long way in fostering a climate of mutual respect and love.

In romantic relationships, gratitude can counter the tendency to take each other for granted. Everyday acts of love and support can easily become invisible over time, leading to a sense of apathy or resentment. Regularly expressing gratitude for these seemingly mundane acts—such as preparing a meal, helping with chores, or offering emotional support—reminds couples of the value they bring to each other's lives.

Furthermore, incorporating intentional acts of gratitude, such as leaving a loving note, preparing a special meal, or gifting a small but meaningful present, can serve as powerful reminders of the love and commitment that binds a couple together. These gestures, infused with gratitude, create a climate of appreciation and deepen the emotional connection between partners. The expression of gratitude is not merely a superficial act, but a conscious effort to actively nurture and maintain the relationship.

The practice of gratitude in relationships, therefore, is not a one-time fix or a quick solution to conflict. It is a continuous process of cultivating awareness, acknowledging the positive, and intentionally expressing appreciation. It requires conscious effort, consistent practice, and a willingness to shift perspective from what is lacking to what is present. It is an investment in the health and longevity of any relationship, strengthening bonds and creating a foundation of mutual respect, love, and understanding that can weather any storm.

The rewards—deeper connections, strengthened bonds, and a more fulfilling life—are immeasurable. The simple act of saying "thank you" becomes a powerful catalyst for transformation, changing the climate of a relationship from one of negativity and resentment to one of appreciation and love. Gratitude fosters greater empathy and understanding, allowing for a nurturing relationship dynamic. When we make gratitude a daily practice,

The Key to a Life of Peace and Purpose

we create an atmosphere of love, respect, and connection that has the power to transform not only our relationships but our entire lives.

CHAPTER FIFTEEN:

BUILDING RESILIENCE THROUGH GRATITUDE

The path of life, while often filled with joy and blessing, is undeniably punctuated by adversity. Challenges, setbacks, and periods of intense difficulty are inevitable. How we navigate these turbulent waters profoundly shapes our character, our faith, and ultimately, our well-being. While it may seem counterintuitive to focus on gratitude during times of hardship, it's precisely in these moments that its power shines most brightly. Gratitude, far from being a naive dismissal of suffering, acts as a potent antidote to despair, fostering resilience and empowering us to face our challenges with strength and unwavering hope.

The Key to a Life of Peace and Purpose

One of the key misunderstandings surrounding gratitude is the notion that it requires ignoring or minimizing suffering. This is a fallacy. True gratitude doesn't demand that we pretend hardship doesn't exist; rather, it encourages us to acknowledge the pain while simultaneously recognizing and appreciating the positive aspects of our lives, even amidst the storm. It's about maintaining a balanced perspective, acknowledging the full spectrum of human experience, the light and the shadow—without allowing the darkness to completely eclipse the light.

Consider the example of a person facing a debilitating illness. The pain and discomfort are undeniable, and the struggle for recovery may seem insurmountable. However, even in this context, opportunities for gratitude exist. It might be gratitude for the support of loved ones, for the skill and dedication of medical professionals, for the simple comfort of a warm bed, or for the strength found within oneself to face each day. These small acts of appreciation, seemingly insignificant in the grand scheme of the illness, collectively create a reservoir of inner strength that fuels perseverance and hope.

Cultivating Gratitude

This is not about trivializing suffering; it's about reframing our perspective. By focusing on what we do have, rather than dwelling on what we lack, we shift our emotional landscape. This doesn't magically erase the pain, but it creates space for hope and resilience to take root. It allows us to find meaning and purpose even in the midst of profound hardship. This balanced perspective is a critical element in building emotional resilience.

Cultivating this perspective requires a conscious and deliberate effort, especially when faced with significant challenges. It's about actively searching for the glimmers of light in the darkness. This might involve reflecting on past blessings, remembering times when you overcame adversity, or focusing on the love and support you receive from others. It could involve appreciating the beauty of nature, the comfort of a warm meal, or the simple joy of human connection.

Adapting our gratitude practice to fit challenging circumstances often requires a shift in focus. In times of ease, our gratitude may focus on the larger aspects of our lives—our family, our health, our career. But during times of hardship, we might need to adjust our lens to appreciate the smaller, seemingly insignificant details. It's in these micro-expressions of gratitude that we find strength. The warmth of the sun on our skin, a kind word from a stranger, a moment of peace and quiet—these are all opportunities to practice gratitude and nurture resilience.

Journaling can be a powerful tool during difficult times. It provides a safe space to process emotions, acknowledge pain, and simultaneously express gratitude for the positive aspects of life. It doesn't require eloquent prose; simply recording a few things you are grateful for each day can have a profound impact on your emotional state. Even on the darkest days, there are likely small things to be thankful for.

Mindful reflection is another powerful tool. Taking a few moments each day to be present in the moment, to observe our surroundings, and to appreciate the simple things can help ground us and foster a sense of calm amidst the chaos. This can be as simple as appreciating the taste of our food, the feeling of the sun on our skin, or the sound of birdsong.

Expressing gratitude to others is crucial. Sharing our appreciation with those who have supported us during challenging times strengthens our bonds and reminds us that we are not alone. A simple thank-you note, a phone call, or a heartfelt conversation can go a long way in both boosting our own spirits and strengthening our relationships.

Furthermore, drawing upon our faith during difficult times is essential. For many, faith provides a source of strength, comfort, and hope that sustains them through periods of adversity. Prayer, meditation, or simply reflecting on scriptures can provide solace and perspective. It is in these moments of quiet contemplation that we can reconnect with our spiritual foundation, find renewal, and draw upon inner reserves of strength. Remember, your faith is a cornerstone of your resilience.

Spiritual practices, such as meditation and prayer, can be profoundly helpful in cultivating gratitude and fostering resilience. Meditation cultivates present-moment awareness, allowing us to focus on the positive aspects of our current experience rather than dwelling on past hurts or future anxieties. Prayer can provide a connection to a higher power, offering comfort, guidance, and a sense of peace that can be incredibly valuable during challenging times. These practices encourage a

The Key to a Life of Peace and Purpose

shift in perspective, from a state of worry and fear to one of acceptance and inner peace.

The integration of gratitude into the healing process after trauma requires a nuanced approach. It's not about minimizing or ignoring the pain experienced, but rather about creating space for hope and healing alongside the acknowledgment of suffering. Trauma, by its very nature, shatters our sense of safety, security, and control. It leaves deep emotional wounds that require time, care, and often professional help to heal. Gratitude, in this context, becomes a tool, not a panacea. It is a vital component in rebuilding a life after trauma, but it's crucial to remember that the healing journey is a personal one, and the pace of progress varies greatly from individual to individual.

Healing from trauma is a deeply personal journey. There is no single path, no prescribed timeline, and no magic solution. What works for one individual may not work for another. The approach should always be individualized and tailored to the unique needs and experiences of each person. While gratitude is a powerful tool, it is just one piece of the puzzle. It must be integrated with other forms of therapeutic intervention, supportive relationships, and self-care strategies to be truly effective. The path toward healing may be arduous and emotionally challenging, but it is a path that leads toward hope, restoration, and a fuller appreciation for life's blessings. This journey demands patience, self-compassion, and an unwavering belief in the potential for healing and growth, a belief that is deeply rooted in faith and resilience. The ultimate goal is not to erase the trauma but to integrate it into the narrative of one's life, to find meaning and purpose amidst the challenges, and to cultivate a future that is filled with hope, gratitude, and a deeper appreciation for life's precious gifts.

CHAPTER SIXTEEN:

LIVING WITH GRATITUDE: A LIFE OF PEACE AND PURPOSE

When we choose to live with gratitude—not as a fleeting feeling, but as a daily posture of the heart—we begin to experience something extraordinary: a life marked by peace and filled with purpose.

Gratitude grounds us. It roots us in the present moment, silencing the relentless pull of regret from the past or anxiety about the future. It reminds us that we are not lacking, not abandoned, and not overlooked. Even when life is uncertain, even when the winds howl and the waves rise, gratitude speaks a better word. It whispers that God is near—that His hand is steady, His provision enough, and His promises unshakable.

This is where we find peace. Not the fragile kind the world offers, easily broken and often tied to circumstance—but the deep, abiding peace that Jesus promised: a peace that surpasses all understanding and guards our hearts and minds (Philippians 4:7). It is peace born from trust—a trust in the One who holds all things together, who numbers the hairs on our heads, who writes our names on the palm of His hand.

As the Apostle Paul wrote,

"And let the peace of Christ rule in your hearts, to which indeed you were called in one body. And be thankful" (Colossians 3:15).

Did you catch that? Gratitude and peace—woven together. A thankful heart becomes fertile soil for peace to flourish. Worry gives way to worship. Fear yields to faith. Our clenched fists open in surrender. And the burdens we carry become lighter, not because they disappear, but because we place them into the hands of a faithful God who walks with us through every valley.

But peace is only one of gratitude's gifts. The other is purpose.

Gratitude clarifies our vision. When we begin to see every breath as a gift, every sunrise as a miracle, every encounter as a divine appointment—we begin to live differently. More intentionally. More joyfully. We realize that we are not here by chance, but by divine design. Our lives, with all their twists and turns, triumphs and trials, are part of a story far greater than our own.

Gratitude gives us eyes to see that our story fits into God's redemptive plan. It awakens us to our calling—to love deeply, to give generously, to serve faithfully, and to shine brightly. We are here to reflect His glory, to carry His compassion, to speak His truth, and to live out His love in a world desperate for hope.

It is gratitude that fuels this purpose. It reminds us why we serve, why we forgive, why we press on when we feel weary. Gratitude breathes life into our daily routines, transforming mundane tasks into acts of worship. It teaches us that every small offering, when given in love, echoes in eternity.

And when gratitude becomes our lifestyle—when it becomes the lens through which we see our circumstances and the language through which we speak our praise—peace becomes our constant companion, and purpose becomes our compass.

We are no longer merely surviving. We are truly living.

We live with a sense of calling, with a heart attuned to the whispers of the Spirit, and with a readiness to give thanks in all things—not because all things are easy, but because in all things, God is good.

This is the beautiful invitation of a grateful life: to wake each morning with wonder, to walk each day with intention, and to rest each night with peace. To live fully, faithfully, fruitfully—not because we have all we want, but because we've come to recognize that in Christ, we already have more than we deserve.

Gratitude doesn't just change our mood. It changes our mission. It opens our hearts, lifts our heads, and sets our feet on solid ground. And it leads us—not only to a life of peace and purpose—

Cultivating Gratitude

but to a life that reflects the very heart of our gracious, generous, and endlessly faithful God.

Let gratitude be your guide, and you will never be without peace or purpose again.

.

CHAPTER SEVENTEEN:

A LIFE MARKED BY GRATITUDE

As we come to the close of this journey, I invite you to pause for a moment—to take a deep breath and reflect on how far you've come. Not just through the pages of this book, but through the seasons of your own life. Gratitude, we've discovered together, is far more than a fleeting feeling or a polite response to kindness. It is a way of seeing, a way of thinking, a way of living.

From the first chapter, we acknowledged that gratitude doesn't erase pain or hardship. It doesn't deny grief, depression, loss, or brokenness. But it *does* change the way we walk through those valleys.

The Key to a Life of Peace and Purpose

It lifts our eyes from what we lack to what we've been given. It anchors us in hope. And it reminds us that even in the storm, God is present—faithful, steady, and full of grace.

We explored how gratitude brings healing, not just to our emotions, but to our spirit. Whether it's through mindfulness, journaling, prayer, or simply noticing the beauty of the present moment, we've learned that gratitude draws us closer to God. It invites us to see His fingerprints in the everyday smile from a friend, a warm breeze, a verse of Scripture that speaks just when we need it most.

We spoke of the power of a grateful heart in relationships—how saying "thank you" can heal wounds, bridge gaps, and build stronger bonds. Whether it's a word spoken to a child, an act of kindness shared with a stranger, or a heartfelt prayer offered on someone's behalf, gratitude ripples outward. It transforms not only us but those around us.

And let us not forget the power of testimony. Through your stories and mine—of illness and healing, failure and redemption, sorrow and restoration—we've seen how gratitude becomes a lifeline. A way through. A declaration of trust in a God who is always working, even when the outcome is

Cultivating Gratitude

still unknown. As I've shared my own journey—through brokenness, prison, and into the arms of grace—I hope you've seen that no pit is too deep, no heart too far gone, that God cannot reach down and restore with His mercy.

We also looked at the discipline of journaling—how the written word can become a sacred record of God's faithfulness. A gratitude journal is not just a notebook. It's a testimony. A legacy. A conversation between your soul and the Savior who walks with you each step of the way.

In these pages, we've learned that gratitude is not about pretending all is well. It is about declaring that God is still good, even when life is hard. It is about trusting that His love is unwavering, His promises are sure, and His mercies are new every morning.

So, where do we go from here?

We live it.

We begin each day with a heart that whispers, *"Thank You, Lord."* We seek the good, speak it aloud, and write it down. We share our appreciation freely—with our families, our coworkers, our neighbors. We learn to say thank you in the quiet places of our hearts, and in the public spaces where others are watching. And when life grows heavy, we

The Key to a Life of Peace and Purpose

return to the well of gratitude—not as a denial of the weight, but as a source of strength to carry it.

Gratitude will not make our lives perfect. But it will make them beautiful.

And here's the most delightful part of all: when we live a life of gratitude, we reflect the heart of Christ. Jesus, who gave thanks before multiplying the bread. Jesus, who lifted His eyes and gave thanks even before raising Lazarus from the grave. Jesus, who, on the night He was betrayed, *gave thanks*—knowing full well the pain that was to come. If He could give thanks then, surely we can give thanks now.

Friend, let this not be the end of the journey— but the beginning of a new way of living. Let your life be marked by thankfulness, your words seasoned with grace, your days filled with quiet joy. Let every moment become an opportunity to praise the One who has walked with you, sustained you, and loved you with an everlasting love.

Thank you for walking this road with me. My heart is full.

Now go—live, cultivate gratitude on a daily basis and discover the peace and purpose God intended for you that can only be revealed by living a grateful life.

Cultivating Gratitude

And never forget...

You are loved.

You are chosen.

You are His.

And for that—we give thanks.

The Key to a Life of Peace and Purpose

Acknowledgements:

I offer my deepest gratitude to God, the Author and Finisher of my faith, whose unwavering love and grace have sustained me through every trial and triumph. This book would not exist without His divine guidance, mercy, and inspiration. To Him be all the glory.

I'd also like to take this opportunity to acknowledge the help of my sisters, Diane, whom you've met through the pages of this book, and Patricia, who've given me sound advice and direction in the writing of this book. Their help, encouragement and prayers help keep me going. Patricia has taken mother's place since her passing as the intercessory prayer warrior for our family. Her faith is infectious!

A special note of heartfelt thanks goes to my son, Benjamin. It was his gentle persistence that led me to attend the life-chang- ing event where God's grace truly broke through, allowing me to fully embrace the forgiveness I had long known in my mind, but struggled to receive in my spirit.

On the first day of the event, we were asked to enter into a covenant of silence for eight hours, finding a place of solitude to be alone with God. As

The Key to a Life of Peace and Purpose

I sat quietly under a tree on a hillside in north Texas, my heart was still wrestling with the very concept of receiving. I knew the truth of 1 John 1:9-that if we confess our sins, God is faithful and just to forgive us and cleanse us from all unrighteousness. Yet despite knowing this in my head, my spirit had not fully embraced it.

That afternoon, I opened my Bible without intent or plan. It fell open to Psalm 32-a passage God had already chosen for me. As I began to read, something broke inside me, and I found my- self weeping uncontrollably. In that sacred moment, I knew that God saw my heart, knew my longing to be fully restored to Him, and lovingly etched His truth into the very walls of my soul. It was there, under that tree, that I finally understood: His grace, forgiveness, and mercy were mine-fully and completely.

These are the words God gave me that day, and they remain written on my heart:

Psalms 32

Blessed is he whose transgression is forgiven, Whose sin is covered.

Cultivating Gratitude

2 Blessed is the man to whom the Lord does not impute iniquity, And in whose spirit there is no deceit.

3 When I kept silent, my bones grew old Through my groaning all the day long.

4For day and night Your hand was heavy upon me; My vitality was turned into the drought of summer. Selah

5 I acknowledged my sin to You, And my iniquity I have not hidden.

I said, "I will confess my transgressions to the Lord," And You forgave the iniquity of my sin. Selah

6 For this cause everyone who is godly shall pray to You In a time when You may be found; Surely in a flood of great waters They shall not come near him.

7You are my hiding place; You shall preserve me from trouble; You shall surround me with songs of deliverance. Selah

8 I will instruct you and teach you in the way you should go; I will guide you with My eye.

9 Do not be like the horse or like the mule,

Which have no understanding, Which must be harnessed with bit and bridle, Else they will not come near you.

The Key to a Life of Peace and Purpose

10 Many sorrows shall be to the wicked;

But he who trusts in the Lord, mercy shall surround him.

11 Be glad in the Lord and rejoice, you righteous; And shout for joy, all you upright in heart!

ABOUT THE AUTHOR

jesse, a servant of Christ, is a passionate communicator, teacher, and encourager who lives each day with a deep sense of gratitude for the grace of God. Having experienced profound personal redemption and restoration, jesse writes from a place of authenticity, humility, and hard-won hope. Now serving full-time in Christian ministry, he devotes his life to encouraging others in their walk with Christ—especially those journeying through seasons of brokenness, doubt, or healing.

With a heart for the hurting and a message grounded in Scripture, jesse weaves personal testimony with biblical truth to help others discover the peace and purpose found in a life of thanksgiving. Cultivating Gratitude is his heartfelt invitation to all who long to live with deeper joy, stronger faith, and a renewed sense of God's presence in every circumstance.

The Key to a Life of Peace and Purpose

Psalms of Thanksgiving

Psalm 100:4-5

Enter into his gates with thanksgiving, and into his courts with praise: be thankful unto him, and bless his name. For the Lord is good; his mercy is everlasting; and his truth endureth to all generations.

Psalm 107:1

O give thanks unto the Lord, for he is good: for his mercy endureth for ever.

Psalm 118:1

O give thanks unto the Lord; for he is good: because his mercy endureth for ever.

Psalm 136:1

O give thanks unto the Lord; for he is good: for his mercy endureth for ever.

Psalm 69:30

I will praise the name of God with a song, and will magnify him with thanksgiving.

Psalm 95:2

Cultivating Gratitude

Let us come before his presence with thanks-giving, and make a joyful noise unto him with psalms.

Psalm 30:12

To the end that my glory may sing praise to thee, and not be silent. O Lord my God, I will give thanks unto thee for ever.

Psalm 9:1

I will praise thee, O Lord, with my whole heart; I will shew forth all thy marvellous works.

Psalm 28:7

The Lord is my strength and my shield; my heart trusted in him, and I am helped: therefore my heart greatly rejoiceth; and with my song will I praise him.

Psalm 92:1

It is a good thing to give thanks unto the Lord, and to sing praises unto thy name, O Most High.

Psalm 105:1

O give thanks unto the Lord; call upon his name: make known his deeds among the people.

The Key to a Life of Peace and Purpose

Psalm 106:1

Praise ye the Lord. O give thanks unto the Lord; for he is good: for his mercy endureth for ever.

Psalm 108:3

I will praise thee, O Lord, among the people: and I will sing praises unto thee among the nations.

Psalm 116:17

I will offer to thee the sacrifice of thanksgiving, and will call upon the name of the Lord.

Psalm 147:7

Sing unto the Lord with thanksgiving; sing praise upon the harp unto our God.

New Testament Teachings on Gratitude

1 Thessalonians 5:18

In every thing give thanks: for this is the will of God in Christ Jesus concerning you.

Philippians 4:6

Cultivating Gratitude

Be careful for nothing; but in every thing by prayer and supplication with thanksgiving let your requests be made known unto God.

Colossians 3:17

And whatsoever ye do in word or deed, do all in the name of the Lord Jesus, giving thanks to God and the Father by him.

Colossians 4:2

Continue in prayer, and watch in the same with thanksgiving.

Ephesians 5:20

Giving thanks always for all things unto God and the Father in the name of our Lord Jesus Christ.

Hebrews 13:15

By him therefore let us offer the sacrifice of praise to God continually, that is, the fruit of our lips giving thanks to his name.

2 Corinthians 9:15

Thanks be unto God for his unspeakable gift.

The Key to a Life of Peace and Purpose

Romans 1:8

First, I thank my God through Jesus Christ for you all, that your faith is spoken of throughout the whole world.

1 Corinthians 1:4

I thank my God always on your behalf, for the grace of God which is given you by Jesus Christ.

2 Thessalonians 1:3

We are bound to thank God always for you, brethren, as it is meet, because that your faith groweth exceedingly, and the charity of every one of you all toward each other aboundeth.

Gratitude in Prayer and Worship

Daniel 2:23

I thank thee, and praise thee, O thou God of my fathers, who hast given me wisdom and might, and hast made known unto me now what we desired of thee: for thou hast now made known unto us the king's matter.

Nehemiah 12:46

Cultivating Gratitude

For in the days of David and Asaph of old there were chief of the singers, and songs of praise and thanksgiving unto God.

1 Chronicles 16:34
O give thanks unto the Lord; for he is good; for his mercy endureth for ever.

Ezra 3:11
And they sang together by course in praising and giving thanks unto the Lord; because he is good, for his mercy endureth for ever toward Israel.

Jonah 2:9
But I will sacrifice unto thee with the voice of thanksgiving; I will pay that that I have vowed. Salvation is of the Lord.

Gratitude in Daily Life

Proverbs 3:5-6
Trust in the Lord with all thine heart; and lean not unto thine own understanding. In all thy

ways acknowledge him, and he shall direct thy paths.*

James 1:17

Every good gift and every perfect gift is from above, and cometh down from the Father of lights, with whom is no variableness, neither shadow of turning.

Romans 8:28

And we know that all things work together for good to them that love God, to them who are the called according to his purpose.

*1 Timothy 4:4-5**

For every creature of God is good, and nothing to be refused, if it be received with thanksgiving: For it is sanctified by the word of God and prayer.

Colossians 3:15

And let the peace of God rule in your hearts, to the which also ye are called in one body; and be ye thankful.

Expressing Gratitude Through Actions**

Cultivating Gratitude

Matthew 25:40
And the King shall answer and say unto them, Verily I say unto you, Inasmuch as ye have done it unto one of the least of these my brethren, ye have done it unto me.

Galatians 6:9-10
And let us not be weary in well doing: for in due season we shall reap, if we faint not. As we have therefore opportunity, let us do good unto all men, especially unto them who are of the household of faith.

Hebrews 6:10
For God is not unrighteous to forget your work and labour of love, which ye have shewed toward his name, in that ye have ministered to the saints, and do minister.

Luke 6:38
Give, and it shall be given unto you; good measure, pressed down, and shaken together, and running over, shall men give into your bosom. For with the same measure that ye mete withal it shall be measured to you again.

The Key to a Life of Peace and Purpose

Acts 20:35

I have shewed you all things, how that so labouring ye ought to support the weak, and to remember the words of the Lord Jesus, how he said, It is more blessed to give than to receive.

www.ingramcontent.com/pod-product-compliance
Lightning Source LLC
Chambersburg PA
CBHW060150130626
46556CB00006B/2571